ABOVE ALL A SHEPHERD
Pope John XXIII

"*Shepherd*, ecce pastor. *A little man, a humble priest, but above all a shepherd.* . . . *Do not look upon your Patriarch as a man of politics, as a diplomat. Look for the shepherd of souls.*"—*From first address of Cardinal Roncalli to the Venetians.*

"*We have at heart in a very special manner Our task as shepherd of the entire flock.* . . . *The central point is the zeal of the Good Shepherd, ready for every sacred undertaking, no matter how daring, straightforward, constant, even unto the supreme sacrifice.*"—*Pope John XXIII on the day of his coronation.*

Above All A Shepherd

Pope John XXIII

••••••••••••••••••

BY

UGO GROPPI

AND

JULIUS S. LOMBARDI

••••••••••••••••••

P. J. KENEDY & SONS · NEW YORK

Nihil obstat: JOSEPH H. BRADY, S.T.D.
Censor Librorum

IMPRIMATUR: ✠ THOMAS A. BOLAND, S.T.D., LL.D.
Archbishop of Newark

Newark, February 5, 1959

B
Joannes XXIII

To the Right Reverend Monsignor John L. McNulty,
President of Seton Hall University
and to
Mother Caroline Jonata, M.F.F.,
Provincial of the Religious Teachers Filippini
two outstanding educators whose generous
understanding and encouragement
have made this book possible

Table of Contents

ACKNOWLEDGEMENTS

The authors wish to acknowledge a debt of gratitude to Cajetan A. Tocco, T.O.P., for his technical advice and assistance in the writing of *Above All A Shepherd*. His knowledge of languages and of ecclesiastical terminology and procedures have greatly facilitated the composition of this work.

The authors also wish to acknowledge a debt of gratitude to Reverend Emilio A. Cardelia for making available to them much useful documentation on Pope John XXIII.

I
● ● ● ● ● ● ● ● ● ● ● ● ● ● ● ●

"I Come from Humble Beginnings"

"Vengo dalla umiltà, e fui educato ad una povertà contenuta e benedetta . . ."

ON THE AFTERNOON of October 28, 1958, Signora Assunta Roncalli Marchesi, who lives in a worker's dwelling in Sesto San Giovanni, province of Milano, at Via Risorgimento 265, went out to buy a liter of milk, as was her daily custom. Accompanied by one of her grandchildren, she went down the stairs, walked unhurriedly a short distance down the street, darting an occasional glance at the shop windows or stopping to greet an acquaintance. One of her hands tightly gripped her shopping bag, the other her grandchild.

After a brief stay at the dairy store, Signora Assunta and the child walked back to the house at a leisurely pace. She climbed the stairs slowly, adjusting her step to that of the child. At the landing of her floor a priest was waiting for her, breathless and in a state of great excitement. He was shouting at her in incomprehensible words. A few moments went by before the bewildered Signora Marchesi realized what it was the excited priest was repeating over and over: "They've made your brother the Pope! Didn't you hear the radio?"

Signora Assunta had not heard the radio because her set had been out of order for the past few days.

At about the same time, at Colombera, a farm property in the outlying section of the village of Brusico, in the township of Sotto il Monte, within the kitchen of an old restored peasant house, Signora Enrica, a niece of the new Pope, was pouring out some rice soup for herself and her old uncles, Alfredo, Saverio, and Giuseppe. The room was modest but neat and orderly. A radio, protected by a cloth of floral design and set on the top of a glass-paned credenza, began to broadcast the news of the events taking place in St. Peter's Square. The square was jammed with hundreds of thousands of persons whose eyes were glued on the ancient chimney of the Sistine Chapel watching for the puffs of smoke to rise upward toward the already darkening sky. Would the smoke again be black?

Thus it was the great news came to one of the two Roncalli houses in Sotto il Monte. An uncle, a brother, had been elected Pope and had taken the name of John XXIII!

Enrica paled as she exclaimed in Bergamasco dialect, "*El ziu!*" (the uncle), while Alfredo shouted excitedly, "*El fradel! el fradel!*" (the brother, the brother). Saverio, who was slightly hard of hearing, was slower to understand what had happened, but in a moment he said: "Oh, the things that Providence can do! My brother, a son of peasants, has become Pope!"

Enrica barely had time to put away the soup bowls and to slip on her good dress when she heard the neighbors storming the front gate, crowding against it so that she feared they would break it down if they were not admitted. But before running out Enrica turned to her uncles and, in her rough and ready Bergamasco speech, warned them: *"Dit na gott!"* (Keep quiet). "Be careful what you say. If you say anything silly, Uncle will scold you, even if he is the Pope!"

All the church bells in the parish were already ringing loudly and joyfully.

There is another house in Sotto il Monte that belongs to a Roncalli, located in the village of Gerole, in which live the sons of the Pope's brother Giuseppe Roncalli. Here too the news came like a bolt out of the blue.

Sotto il Monte is a little commune, or township, of two thousand souls in the province of Bergamo, lying at the foot of the steep hill of San Giovanni. Made up of a group of small villages its houses extend from the ancient rocky core of the settlement toward the Adda River, and are bordered by a green frame of fields, meadows, and vineyards. In one of the oldest of these houses, located in the village of Brusico, Angelo Giuseppe Roncalli was born on November 25, 1881.

He was the second of the nine children of Giovanni Battista and Marianna Mazzola. His father was a sharecropper who worked on the farm of Count Ottavio Moriani before he himself became the proprietor of a small plot of land and an independent working farmer.

The old farmhouse in which Angelo was born today is part of a newly constructed farmers' building which stands on the still undivided Roncalli property. His three surviving brothers live there and work in the fields. Today the family of Angelo Giuseppe Roncalli consists of Saverio (75 years old), married but childless; Alfredo (69), a bachelor; Giuseppe (64), a widower with five sons and five daughters; and Assunta, known as the "widow Marchesi," who lives now with one of her four children, a daughter, in Sesto San Giovanni.

The Roncalli family is a very ancient one and divided into several branches. They came to Sotto il Monte as early as 1429, from Valle Imagna, one of the most beautiful valleys in all Lombardy. The branch of the Roncalli family that settled in Sotto il Monte is called Maitini: "Martinus Roncalli dictus Maitinus" was their ancestor. Other families with the same name can be found in the province of Bergamo and here and there in other regions of Italy, and they all originated in Bergamo or Valle Imagna. There are families named Roncalli even in France, and they too came originally from Bergamo.

A study of the various branches of the Roncallis, in Bergamo and elsewhere, discloses that its descendants have belonged to different social strata: monks, priests, doctors, painters. As far as is known they were all people of deep religious faith, simple and unaffected in manner, honest, peaceful and hard working.

Among the closest relatives of the Holy Father, that is the children of his brothers and two sisters, some are laborers and others farmers. One nephew, Don Battista Roncalli, is a young priest of 30 and curate of a parish in

Fusignano in the diocese of Faenza. A niece, a sister of
Don Battista, is a nun in the order of "The Daughters of
Our Lady of the Sacred Heart of Jesus of Issoudun" in
Rome, and another niece, Suor Maria Anna, has been a
religious for almost ten years, belonging to the "Pious
Mothers of the African Missions of Verona." She is
stationed in Asmara, Africa.

Angelo Giuseppe Roncalli has never forgotten his
peasant origins. Years later when he became Patriarch of
Venice and spoke for the first time in the Basilica of St.
Mark, resplendent with its noble columns and glowing
mosaics, he recalled that he was a son of poor people:

"I come from humble beginnings, and I was raised in
a restraining, blessed poverty whose needs are few and
which protects the growth of the highest and noblest
virtues, and prepares one for the great ascents of life."

On the evening of October 28, 1958, when he uttered
his first words as Pope, his thoughts again went back to
the mountains and fields of Sotto il Monte, and to his
father who had died so many years ago, and he said:

"I shall be called John, a name that is sweet to Us because it once was the name of Our father, a name which
is dear to Us because it is the name of the humble parish
in which We received Our baptism."

In that solemn hour when the mere thought of the responsibilities that weigh on the Vicar of Christ drives
the one who is about to assume them to anguish and
bewilderment, Angelo Giuseppe Roncalli found peace
and courage by trusting himself to God and by turning
his thoughts to his distant childhood and his family—
to his mother, dead for many years but ever alive in his

memory, to his father, bent over the rocky soil, and to his aging brothers, who still work in the fields.

At that very twilight hour his distant birthplace, nestled at the foot of the green hills of San Giovanni, was alive with festive music, brilliant with gaily-colored lights, and reverberating to the sound of bursting fire-crackers and shouts of joy. In Rome, in the Sistine Chapel, facing the College of Cardinals and before the whole of the Christian world, Angelo Giuseppe Roncalli ascended the throne of Peter, under the majestic murals that Michelangelo had painted on its ceiling, and before "The Last Judgment" which the genius of Michelangelo, inspired by Dante's vision, had left as a terrible warning to posterity.

Glory? The Pope did not seek it, but he accepted his duty. Out of a true and deep sense of humility he did not choose as a model a pontificate marked by a name gloriously consecrated in history. Since he could not be a Pope without a name, he chose one that was the most common among his predecessors, as if to say: I wish only to be father and shepherd.

"We choose," he said, "a name which in the very ancient series of Roman Pontiffs has the primacy of plurality. . . . We prefer to cover the littleness of Our name with this magnificent succession."

Angelo Giuseppe Roncalli was baptized on November 25, 1881. This is what his brother Giuseppe says of that day:

"It was the morning of November 25, 1881, and they immediately took him to the baptismal font as was the custom in those days. But the pastor wasn't there, he arrived late in the evening. It rained very hard that day and by the time he was baptized it was already night."

Giuseppe, of course, had not yet been born but he had heard the story of that day so often that he told it as though he had himself been present.

Saverio Roncalli, an uncle, was the godfather. The certificate of baptism, preserved in the parish archives, reads: "In the year 1881, on the 25th day of November, I, Francesco Rebuzzini, pastor of this church of San Giovanni Battista of Sotto il Monte, have this day baptized a child born of Giovanni Battista Roncalli and Marianna Mazzola, legally man and wife, of the village of Brusico of this parish, to whom was given the name of Angelo Giuseppe."

After the rite his uncle Saverio raised the child in his arms before the altar of the Virgin, and consecrated him to Our Lady.

When he was the Patriarch of Venice Angelo Roncalli returned every summer to the scenes of his childhood. Each year on the 15th of August a Cardinal of the Holy Roman Church, wearing his *cappa magna*, followed the little Marian procession that was held on that date in his native town. This was a gift that he never failed to make to his fellow parishioners on the occasion of the feast of the Assumption.

His was an abiding interest in the joyful and sorrowful events in the lives of his fellow townsmen, and he was ever ready to comfort them and convince them that he was still the same "Don Angelo" they had known before. This was a source of great joy to him. During his brief sojourns in his native village he would celebrate Mass in his modest private chapel, frequently attended by some pupils from the primary school. At the end of Mass, he would ask the name of each pupil and inquire whether he knew the name of the saint of the day, following which he would relate some biographical details of the saint's life.

During these visits to Sotto il Monte he lived in the modest house at Colombera. From its windows could be seen the countryside sloping down toward the plain of Brianza, between the Adda and the Brembo. There beyond the river was the place where as a child he rode in a little cart accompanied by his parents. His eyes would linger on the church of the Madonna of the Woods and on Somasca, for many years the scene of the labors of a saint dear to him—Jerome Miani, founder of the Somaschi congregation for the care of orphans and abandoned children and who himself had worked so often among the peasants in those fields. Beyond the mountains was the goal of many hikes in his boyhood: the historic Abbey of Pontida, where eight centuries before the Lombard commune had united in a defensive league against the German emperor Barbarossa.

This panorama conjured up memory after memory. A short distance away from the house in which he was born rose the little Franciscan convent of Baccanello. When at noon the friars rang their ancient bell, his mother would always say, "It's time to put the pot on the fire."

The fare on the table in the Roncalli household was of the simplest; meat, wine or sweets were lacking. In the morning there was some mush, or the "national dish" of Bergamo, *polenta,* both made of cornmeal. At noon and in the evening there would be soup and a little cheese and salad.

"We were poor but happy," Cardinal Roncalli often recalled, "and we never were aware of lacking anything. And in truth we lacked nothing; ours was a dignified and contented poverty."

In the village of Corna in Sotto il Monte, which is most inaccessible and out of the way because it sits on a steep hill, there lives an eighty-six-year-old man who remembers Angelo as a boy. Giovanni Bonalumi recalls how they worked together in the fields, and how they would climb up the steep flanks of the hills together with little Angelo tightly holding his hand for fear of slipping. Now Bonalumi deplores the fact that after fifty years of faithful work he is a retired bell-ringer, too old to have rung the bells on the memorable evening of Pope John's election.

At the age of six, Angelo was registered in the elementary school of Sotto il Monte. Every morning, his cloth bookbag under his arm, he would walk the mile and a quarter which separated his house from the communal school. The mile and a quarter became almost two miles after elementary school, when the boy used to go to the parish priest of Carvico in order to carry on his secondary studies.

One of Angelo's former schoolmates still lives in Brusico. Battista Agazzi, called Battistel, is eighty years old, and he was in the third grade when little Roncalli was in

the first. According to his recollection Angelo was a
bright pupil. "Roncalli always understood things
quickly. Although he was only in the first grade, he was
smarter than any of us in the third. And it was evident,"
he adds, "that he would become a success."

It is not to be denied that the reality of today colors
the old peasant's memory of the past. This is human.
The truth is that the school records tell a different story.
It seems that little Angelo, notable for firmness of character and goodness, was not too distinguished in his
studies. Later, at Celana, one of his teachers, following a
severe reprimand, handed him a letter for his pastor who
had recommended him to the school. In this letter the
teacher requested the priest to call the boy to order because he had appeared totally unprepared at the latest
oral examinations. Angelo sensed the contents of the
letter, however, and took care not to deliver it to the
addressee.

The boy's gifts were hidden, but someone did manage
to discover them. This person was the very parish priest
of Carvico—the addressee of the undelivered letter—
who began to initiate the boy into the mysteries of
Latin grammar. Little Roncalli became a non-resident
student at the ancient diocesan institute of Celana, a
small city in the direction of Pontida in the valley of San
Martino and a three-hour walk from Sotto il Monte. He
made this hike every day until his vocation to the priesthood had become apparent.

During the first years of his life, he lived with his
parents, helping them with the heavy farm work since

he was the oldest of the male children. Giovanni Battista early felt that moral support from the boy which is a comfort to fathers and which, perhaps more than material support, unites them almost in a brotherly sense with their sons. He was a rough worker but underneath his leathery face, scorched dry by the sun, Angelo discerned treasures of wisdom and tenderness which he never forgot. His mother and father set him the example of a simple but deep faith, a faith that above all was lived: this was the first and most fundamental teaching that he received from his family.

On the evening of his coronation as Pope, November 4, 1958, John XXIII received his fellow villagers and the faithful of the diocese of Venice who had come by the thousands to witness the ceremony. This audience was a memorable one because of the human warmth which the Pope knew how to infuse in his words, and for the response which he aroused in the hearts of his hearers. In that conversation—he did not want to make a speech—he again spoke of the scenes of his childhood and of his distant diocese on the Venetian lagoon, almost as if he were taking leave of them. He recalled one day when he was seven years old and when his father had carried him on his shoulders for several miles to attend a meeting of the Catholic Action organization. His spiritual journey, he said, had begun then—a journey in the service of God and man which had continued for seventy years.

The inhabitants of the Bergamasco region are frank, open-hearted Christians, of elementary but deeply implanted virtues, firm and steadfast in their sense of duty.

These qualities have made the region, once subject to the rule of the old "serene" Republic of Venice, a fortress of Catholicism in Italy. Bergamo has given many ecclesiastics of great piety and learning to the Church, and today in the Roman Curia and in the diplomatic service of the Holy See Bergamasco prelates like Mons. Gustavo Testa, the Apostolic Nuncio to Berne; Mons. Pietro Sigismondi, Secretary of the Congregation for the Propagation of the Faith, and Mons. Giacomo Testa, Apostolic Delegate to Turkey, give honor to the Church and to their native region.

Religious vocations are numerous in this region and Angelo soon heard a voice calling him to leave the good earth of his father's farm, so that he might toil in another vineyard: he wanted to go to the seminary. His parents needed him, but they were Christians and felt that with that call the Lord was blessing their home.

He was thirteen years old when he entered the seminary of Bergamo. At fourteen he began to wear the clerical garb, and from that moment on his parents and brothers no longer used the familiar "thou" (*tu*) with him but the more formal "you" (*voi*).

Even at the seminary it appears that he did not immediately manifest the intellectual gifts that were his. As sometimes happens to persons endowed with a strong personality and who live in an inner world of their own, he made a poor adjustment to a program of studies that was rigidly fixed both in subject matter and methods. Already as a child Angelo had his own private inner world in which his fancy roamed free under the stimulus of the little events of every day with their joys and

sorrows. Perhaps it was a great effort for one of his disposition, accustomed to the freedom of nature, to submit
to a rigid discipline. But the voice that had originally
called him, together with a tenacious will, led him to
overcome these external difficulties.

Little by little, Angelo was able to bring his native
gifts into harmony with the canons of the ecclesiastical
ratio studiorum. And little by little the lively intelligence he had manifested before entering the seminary
became disciplined, while his piety grew to be exemplary. He gradually forged his own true character; his
will triumphed without stultifying his intelligence. He
began to distinguish himself in his studies and helped his
companions to overcome the obstacles that were already
behind him. It was at this time that he developed a taste
for humanistic studies which he has never lost.

On June 28, 1895, he received his first tonsure. The
following year he became a dormitory prefect, and in
1898 he received minor orders.

It was while he was still at the Bergamo seminary that
young Angelo Roncalli served his obligatory stint in the
army—between 1899 and 1901. An old army comrade
of his still lives in Martinengo, not far from Bergamo.
Giovanni Manenti, now 79, will tell anyone who cares to
listen that he knew the soldier Angelo Roncalli. Manenti
was called to the colors with the same class and was assigned to the 78th Infantry Regiment with headquarters
in Bergamo in the Umberto I Barracks. He recalls that
he was in the same outfit with Roncalli for six months
and that he used to make his cot for him. Roncalli was
always absent at the time of ration distribution since, as

a student, he was free to leave the barracks. In exchange for making his cot, he authorized Manenti to receive his rations. It seems that Don Angelo was an excellent instructor of recruits, because his platoon was always among the best in the battalion.

In September 1901 he was discharged from the service, free to return to his studies at the seminary. After receiving his diploma he was sent to complete his studies in philosophy and theology in the Pontifical Roman Seminary where he was to receive the degree of Doctor of Sacred Theology. Angelo Roncalli received one of the seven scholarships to the Roman Seminary which have been available to natives of Bergamo ever since the Seminary absorbed the ancient Cerasoli College. This at one time was the scholastic center for Bergamasco students in Rome.

At that time the seat of this Pontifical Roman Seminary was not at the Lateran, as it is now. It was then located in the heart of old Rome between Via della Scrofa, Piazza Sant' Agostino and that street which today is called Via Santa Giovanna d'Arco. About it were many other little streets which have disappeared as a result of the demolitions that have opened up the Corso del Rinascimento. The massive building was linked by a still existing street-arch to an adjacent structure which includes the Church of Sant' Apollinare. This was the location—up to about thirty years ago—of the Apollinare, the university of canon and civil law.

The two massive structures, not devoid of nobility in their architectural lines, are still there. But the old, quaint Rome that surrounded these buildings with its colorful and noisy population, its narrow streets, village-like public squares, taverns crowded with coachmen while their skinny, underfed horses waited outside, its singing and gesticulating street vendors, has irretrievably vanished. Palazzo Madama, the Italian house of Senators, is nearby, and the Italian house of Parliament, Montecitorio, is not far away. Beyond the Tiber lie St. Peter's and the Vatican. The charm of old Rome, in part vanished, consists of these contrasts between the grandiose and the plebeian.

It was in these buildings that Angelo Roncalli spent the years of his most intensive preparation for the priesthood. Those days were recalled when, on November 27, 1958, Pope John XXIII returned to the seminary which he had left fifty years before. He was received in the main hall where he engaged in intimate conversation with the professors and students. His words were tinged with a moving nostalgia as the new Pope spoke of persons and places of the past, now dearer than ever to him either because they were no more or had radically changed. These are from his unedited words as transcribed by a tape-recorder:

"Ah, life has become very long; how many years . . . have passed since We left the Seminary! . . . Once again I see those surroundings, those staircases, those halls and the chapel. I see our superiors, Mons. Bugarini —oh, Mons. Bugarini! The bursar Garroni who used to pass us in the refectory saying, 'Don't eat too much! Don't eat too much!'—One would think that the responsibility for the provisions of the entire city weighed on him. . . . And our Vice Rector, and later Rector,

Spolverini, whom we loved but also feared a little, but whom we always esteemed. . . .

"And then there was the Professor of Church History, Mons. Benigni, who had a speech impediment but who in his fine lectures found a vibrant voice for the expression of his ideas. Occasionally he would interrupt his lectures in order to correct the proofs of the *Voce della Verità* which was published in the basement of the Altemps building. And once he broke the silence to exclaim: 'Oh, a serious incident, a serious incident! They have killed King Alexander of Serbia together with Queen Draga! Thus we came to know what was going on in the world, even though it was forbidden to us to read newspapers, even the *Osservatore Romano*.

"We used to gather in the chapel of the Madonna della Fiducia. In the summers an excellent preacher, a Jesuit, would talk to us about the eternal truths. And if he were talking about Purgatory, he would shout 'Fire! Fire!' This would bring the barber and other shopkeepers in the stores below running into the Piazza Sant'Apollinare.

"And Padre Francesco [1]—must I not also remember Padre Francesco? If later we did make something of our lives, we must say it came from him. . . . And I shall not say anything about the beautiful songs that the present Mons. Tardini sang for us because he was considered, we will not say a great singer, but a tenor of the first rank."

[1] Father Francesco Pitocchi, C.SS.R., spiritual director of the seminary, who died in 1922 with a reputation for saintliness and whose cause of beatification has been introduced. According to some persons, Father Pitocchi predicted to the young seminarian from Bergamo that one day he would mount the Chair of Peter.

Thus did Pope John XXIII simply and informally recall a distant but not forgotten world.

At the end of his studies Angelo Roncalli was ordained a priest. In his own words, "These two dates—the tenth and eleventh of August—mark the beginning of the fiftieth year of my priesthood: August 10, 1904, my priestly ordination in Rome in the Church of Santa Maria in Montesanto on Piazza del Popolo at the hands of His Excellency, Mons. Ceppetelli, patriarch of Constantinople and vice-gerent of Rome; August 11th, my first Mass in the basilica of St. Peter's on the tomb of the Apostle, followed by the blessing of the Holy Father, Pius X, in the Vatican—which he gave with his hands on my head—and his saintly, unforgettable words."

He himself recalled these dates to his faithful in Venice at the beginning of his Jubilee Year in order to ask them "to abstain from any liturgical, academic, verbal, epistolary, public or private manifestation." The memory of those distant days was enough for him: it sufficed to remember those moments when, prostrate on the floor of the little church in the Piazza del Popolo, he had become a priest. It was enough for him to recall the white figure and the gentle words of Saint Pius X, who had encouraged the young priest from Bergamo and expressed the hope that his priesthood would be a great consolation to the Church of God.

Following his ordination he remained in Rome for about a month. In January 1905 he had an encounter which may well have changed the course of his life. This story was told shortly after the election of Cardinal Roncalli as Supreme Pontiff, by one of his contemporaries, Mons. Guglielmo Carozzi, who had studied with him at the Roman major seminary and who is now arch-priest in Seriate:

". . . I wept when I heard the news on the radio two hours ago. My thoughts went far back to January 29, 1905, when in the same Sistine Chapel where he was elected today, I witnessed the consecration of Mons. Radini-Tedeschi as Bishop of Bergamo at the hands of St. Pius X. The two Bergamasco priests, students at the Roman Seminary, who assisted at the altar during the Papal Mass were Angelo Roncalli and myself. When several days later, just before Bishop Radini was leaving for Bergamo to take possession of his episcopal see, he asked the rector of the Roman Seminary if he could recommend a Bergamasco priest to act as his secretary. Don Angelo was the rector's choice. The rector recommended him because he was 'more Romanized.' Since that choice, made 52 years ago, a ray of light has accompanied this predestined priest. It was the schooling of Mons. Radini that embarked him on that road which today led back to Rome, as if completing a circle."

In order to understand what the memory of Bishop Radini-Tedeschi means to Angelo Roncalli it suffices perhaps to mention two particulars. In the house at Sotto il Monte to which the Cardinal Patriarch of Venice returned every year, are preserved the white *zucchetto* of Leo XIII and the violet-colored one once worn by Mons. Radini-Tedeschi. They are kept in an urn among the books and papers in his study. It has been observed that this modest glass urn contains, as it were, the indications of the providential path marked out by God, for Angelo Giuseppe Roncalli.

The other particular is the following: At the moment of his election the Cardinal Patriarch of Venice was wearing the purple robe bequeathed to him as a precious legacy by his never-forgotten Bishop. Mons. Giacomo Radini-Tedeschi had worn it for the first time in that very same Sistine Chapel when he had received the episcopal consecration from the hands of St. Pius X.

II

•••••••••••••••

Under A Great Master

Bishop Giacomo Maria Radini-Tedeschi

GIACOMO MARIA of the aristocratic family of the
Counts Radini-Tedeschi was born in Piacenza on July
12, 1857, the second of six children of Count Carlo
Radini-Tedeschi and Luisa Pantini, of Genoese origin.
The tradition of the family was deeply religious: two
paternal uncles, Gaetano and Camillo, were Jesuits who
were held in high esteem by the Society. Two aunts,
Diana and Marianna, were nuns of the Institute of the
Ursuline Ladies of Piacenza which Giacomo's younger
sister, Maria Felice, was to enter later, eventually becoming its prioress. A cousin of his father was a canon of
the cathedral, and a maternal uncle was a canon of the
metropolitan cathedral of Genoa.

Giacomo's childhood years were spent serenely in a
climate of deep Christian piety. He made his first studies
in his native city in a school run by the Brothers of the
Christian Schools whose house was near the Radini-
Tedeschi residence. In 1866 he became a pupil in the

Paganini College of Genoa where he remained until 1870 when the school was closed. He was then transferred, along with his brothers Prospero and Giuseppe, to the College of Sant' Alessandro in Bergamo and entrusted to the care of a pious priest, Mons. Alessandro Valsecchi, who at that very time had been nominated titular bishop of Tiberiade and coadjutor of Mons. Speranza, Bishop of Bergamo.

Those were difficult days for the diocese. As has been said, Bergamo is one of the most Catholic cities in Italy. The new Italian government considered Mons. Speranza to be pro-Austrian—the Austrian government had recommended him to the Holy See for his post—and the anti-clerical liberal factions looked upon the diocese as "mission country" to be won over to the national cause. Government officials, therefore, did everything possible to make life difficult for the Bishop and Catholic institutions. Even the College of Sant' Alessandro was not spared administrative vexations and its students were systematically discriminated against by the government examiners before whom they had to appear.

Such a situation could but influence young Giacomo who began to understand that religion is not only a treasure that is possessed but one that must also be defended. In the summer of 1876 he obtained his licentiate's diploma. The young man wanted to enter a seminary but his father wished him to serve his period of army service before assuming the clerical garb. So from 1876–77 he took courses in theology as a non-resident student and in civilian dress at the diocesan seminary of Piacenza.

He was, however, exempted from military service because of poor health and it thus became possible for him to don the cassock and continue his studies toward his vocation. After finishing his second year in theology, he went on to the Pontifical Lombard Seminary in Rome, completing his studies in theology and canon law at the Gregorian University. In the summer of 1879 he obtained a degree in theology in Genoa and in the following year he took a degree in canon and civil law in Rome.

He was ordained as a priest on November 2, 1879, by the Bishop of Piacenza, Mons. Gian Battista Scalabrini. The same bishop assigned him in the following year to teach canon law in the seminary of Bedonia. A year later the young priest was teaching canon law in the seminary of Piacenza where he remained for ten years. During this period he published studies on the law of concordats and the temporal power of the Church which aroused lively discussion not only in Italy but in other countries.

At the same time he dedicated himself to his pastoral duties. "It was at Piacenza," wrote Mons. Roncalli in his biography of Bishop Radini-Tedeschi, "that the first period of Mons. Radini's industrious priesthood began in 1881. Here he immediately attracted the attention and sympathy of his fellow-citizens, surprised to see a young patrician of elegant manners, as well as one so highly talented and cultured, dedicate himself to the ministry of souls by preaching, listening to penitents, and by attending to all kinds of tasks, even the most humble, in which he could be useful."

Don Giacomo Radini-Tedeschi also devoted himself actively to the apostolate of charity in the work of the Conferences of St. Vincent de Paul, and was an ardent promoter of this work within and outside his diocese. Almost at the same time, in 1883, he made his first pilgrimage to Lourdes. There he came to the notice of Count Aquaderni, one of the pioneers of Catholic Action in Italy, who asked that he be assigned to the national organization sponsoring pilgrimages, a work to which the young priest gave a decisive impetus.

As he himself explained in a speech, these pilgrimages had two meanings for him. First, that of reawakening the idea of the supernatural which had been weakened by the then rampant positivism; second to "open the way to faith, but to a practical faith, which finds concrete expression in good works and Christian observance." For him the pilgrimages were a weapon of the apostolate, a means of accelerating the spiritual renewal of Italy; in a word, the forerunner of Catholic Action that was rightly inspired and spiritually fruitful.

He had already been a member of Catholic Action proper since 1882 when he had been called to participate in the work of the congresses which summoned Catholics to organize in efficient apostolic action in filial union with the ecclesiastical hierarchy. It was in this period that the young priest Giacomo Radini-Tedeschi underwent experiences which had a great educational value for him.

The history of Italian Catholicism in the second half of the nineteenth century and in the first decades of the present century is a stormy one. When the Pope lost his temporal power on September 20, 1870, Catholics, faithful to the directions of Pius IX and his successor, abstained from any participation in the political life of the country. They did not even exercise their right to vote because they could not, even indirectly, appear to be approving the violent expropriation of which the Church had been a victim. A painful period opened for Catholics: they could not but love the country of their birth and desire its moral and civil progress. But at the same time they could not forget that a great injustice had been done to the Church.

A grave consequence of their keeping away from the polls, counseled and commanded by the Church (*the non expedit*),[1] was that the first laws of the new Italy were formulated by the representatives of minorities who were enemical or ill disposed toward the Church, or imbued with a secularism often leading to outbursts of anti-clericalism.

Damaging as this was for the Catholic cause, the political abstention continued for several years. On the part of some Catholics it was a desire to return to the old order of things but for the majority it was an expression of loyalty to the Church and to the Vicar of Christ. The real and deep reason for the *non expedit* is different from that cited by liberal non-Catholic or anti-Catholic historians. For a millennium the whole Catholic world had viewed the temporal power of the Pope as a guarantor of the independence of the Church, and therefore as a prerequisite of her universality.

[1] "It is not expedient," Pope Pius IX had said, "that Catholics vote . . ."

Today, almost a century later, it is easy to say that such fears were unfounded, but between 1860 and 1880 it was a commonly held opinion that deprived of temporal power the Church would disintegrate. Declared enemies of Catholicism—among them Giuseppe Mazzini—were certain that, once the Papal States were occupied by unified Italy, Catholicism would rapidly decline and disappear. The reports of the Austrian ambassador to the Vatican, after September 20, 1870, referred to the Curia as though it were an old broken-down watch whose mechanism was slowing up and which would soon stop forever.

Catholics who have the certainty of the divine promise knew that the Church could not fail in her mission, but they also knew from history that she was not immune to grave trials.

The reserve of the Holy See toward a united Italy was an act of religious, not political defense. What would have happened if, after the violent expropriation of papal property, the Pope had accepted it as a *fait accompli* and Catholics had tranquilly integrated themselves into the new Italian political structure? In the eyes of the world would the Pope not have seemed to be a mere Italian bishop, an instrument in the hands of the new political power installed in Rome? In that case was it not possible that the Apostolic Roman Church might become an Italian national church?

The firm and repeated protests of Pius IX and his immediate successors, the political abstention of Italian Catholics were not, therefore, expressions of resentment over the loss of a material good, but attitudes imposed by the duty of preserving for the Church, in external form, her universal character. The *non expedit*, however, did have negative consequences for Italian Catholicism, the weight of which is still being felt. An isolation lasting almost seventy years is bound to have such effect, but it was a tribute that had to be paid to the universalism of the Church.

Nonetheless, Italian Catholics did not remain inactive during those years. Spurred on by the Popes, they gave themselves to a religious and social apostolate, to a form of Catholic Action which bent its efforts to renew society in Christ, by living their faith openly professed, day by day, and by testifying to it with good works. In 1875 Italian Catholic organization was centered around the *Opera dei Congressi* (Work of the Congresses) and around Catholic committees directed by a permanent central committee connected with parallel diocesan and parochial structures.

At first the orientation of the *Opera* was one of passive resistance, but under Leo XIII its attention was directed to the urgent solution of social problems. The very critical attitude of Italian Catholics toward the Italian State led them to stress serious economic and social shortcomings which weighed down especially on the working classes. Apart from this human consideration, there was another reason for inducing them to concern themselves actively with labor problems. This was the spread of atheistic socialism among the working classes. The workers were falling away from religion, and hence it was deemed necessary that religion go to them.

By 1891 when the encyclical *Rerum novarum* was promulgated there were already 289 Catholic worker societies, most of them of a mutual aid character, with about 75,000 members. There were more than 700 rural credit unions for poor peasants. The year 1895 saw the first efforts to build Christian trade unions under the name of Secretariats of the People.

Giacomo Radini-Tedeschi was in Piacenza at the beginning of the pontificate of Leo XIII. When the Pope asked Italian Catholics to unite their forces for the common cause of Catholic Action and to abandon sterile discords, some of those who wished to remain aloof from all forms of public and social action were disillusioned. The so-called intransigents would have preferred an unconditional approval of their attitudes and, at the same time, that a rebuke be administered to their adversaries. Mons. Gian Battista Scalabrini, the Bishop of Piacenza, became the target of these elements who, directly or indirectly, accused him of "liberalism." They were supported by a Catholic newspaper published in Milan, *L'Osservatore Cattolico*, which did not spare the Bishop from attack or criticism.

The "intransigents" tried the coup of balancing the attitudes of Cardinal Pitra, a ranking member of the Sacred College, against those of Leo XIII. The former, at the invitation of a Flemish newspaper, wrote a letter in which he exalted the greatness of the pontificate of Pius IX, almost completely ignoring his successor. In fact, he compared the times to those of the anti-Christ. This was symptomatic of a tendency which appears now and then in the Catholic world: namely, trying to teach the Pope what he should and what he should not do.

Cardinal Pitra's letter was exploited by the intransigents who used it as a pretext for publishing and disseminating an anonymous pamphlet which might have produced a deep confusion, especially among the clergy. Protests and attestations of devotion to Leo XIII poured in from every quarter. Mons. Scalabrini went even further: he put his clergy on guard against the pamphlet and at the same time exhorted them to greater devotion to the Pope. Shortly after, he in turn published a pamphlet, *Intransigents and Transigents*, under the byline, "An Italian Bishop." Quite unexpectedly this pamphlet was disapproved by the Holy See, perhaps for the reason that it did not wish to provoke harmful internal polemics. The fact remains that the Bishop was embittered and that in his diocese only more fuel was added to the discussions for and against Mons. Scalabrini.

What during this time was the attitude of Don Giacomo Radini-Tedeschi? He had been educated by the "intransigents" and he was one of them. But he was one of them in a correct and honest way, and by always most strictly observing ecclesiastical discipline and by revising his own position when this seemed to him necessary. He was a just man and not a factionalist. For this reason he felt that the milieu around Piacenza was no longer for him.

It was just at this time that the Pope, to whom he had been presented by the directors of the *Opera dei Congressi*, summoned him to the Pontifical Ecclesiastical

Academy in Rome[2] where the diplomats of the Holy
See were trained. He was more of a guest than a student
at the Academy because as soon as he arrived in Rome
he was assigned as a *minutante* in the Secretariat of State.
Of this period (1890–6) Mons. Roncalli wrote:

". . . One day in 1896 the great Pontiff sent for the
young priest—he was thirty-nine—and told him about
his plan to send him to Belgium as apostolic nuncio. His
answer was as humble and respectful as it was prompt
and frank: *'Holy Father, I am not and do not wish to
be a diplomat, my lips immediately say the est-est and
the non-non of the Gospel, but in diplomacy . . .'*"

Mons. Roncalli continued: "In reality he possessed
uncommon gifts for success as a diplomat of great value.
Those who knew him in Rome, including the most authoritative persons, repeated this over and over again.
A short while before he had also excused himself from
accepting the archbishopric of Bucharest in Rumania
where Cardinal Ledochowski wanted him at any cost,
hoping it would bring great advantages to the cause of
Catholicism in a region where at that time the situation
was difficult and complex. His noble and frank attitude,
so edifying before the mirage of earthly honor and
greatness which would have been a temptation even
for ecclesiastics more austere than he, ended by winning him the complete affection of the great pontiff. As
a proof of his benevolence Leo XIII had already sent
him to Vienna in 1891 as ablegate to bring the red hat
to the new Cardinal Gruscha, Archbishop of that city.
And in 1893 he sent him to Paris on a similar mission

[2] At that time it was called the Academy of Noble Ecclesiastics.

to Cardinal Bourret, Archbishop of Rodez. On both occasions the young monsignor was accompanied by Dr. Achille Ratti. . . ."

After thus renouncing a diplomatic career, in 1896 Don Giacomo Radini-Tedeschi was appointed canon of Santa Maria Maggiore and a few months later, at the beginning of 1897, he was transferred to the chapter of the Vatican Basilica. From this moment he dedicated himself to the priestly ministry, to Catholic Action, and to the organization of pilgrimages to Lourdes and Palestine. An eloquent orator, words were a valuable weapon to him in this apostolate and he won a national reputation throughout Italy as a preacher and giver of retreats. He had been prominent at all Catholic Congresses since 1891 and in all of them, from the one in Vicenza in 1891 to the one in Bologna in 1901, his eloquence fired souls and inspired them to action.

In Rome, where he conducted the tireless ministry for about fifteen years, he was assiduous in his duties as a director at the Sodality of the Immaculate Virgin, and at the same time he was active in welfare activities of all kinds. And it should not be forgotten that he was the first teacher of Christian sociology in the Leonine Institute.

A great organizer, Mons. Radini-Tedeschi was in charge of religious assistance to pilgrims during the Holy Year in 1900. In 1904 he played an active role in preparing for the jubilee feasts in connection with the fifteenth anniversary of the proclamation of the dogma of the Immaculate Conception.

His activity in the cause of Catholic Action continued

unabated. In 1898, following socialist disorders in Milan, the liberal government unleashed a merciless policy of repression that also affected Catholics. The local police authorities knew very well that Catholics had not engaged in any seditious activity, but the government feared these forces and seized this opportunity to dissolve many associations, thereby undermining the *Opera dei Congressi* which at that time was presided over by Count Paganuzzi of Venice. The vice president was Mons. Radini-Tedeschi.

Paganuzzi's authoritarian character and centralizing tendencies, together with the circumstances created by the repressions in Milan and the legalized violence of the government sowed confusion among Catholics. Differences, which had been latent for some time, arose in the Congress between the older and younger people. The President was determined to maintain an attitude of firm intransigence against any tendency which appeared dangerous only because it was new. The younger people were acutely aware of the march of events in the world and of the impossibility of closing one's eyes before the new reality. Those years saw the rise of the first Christian Democratic movement, inspired by generous intentions but not always wisely conducted. In the face of what appeared to be the dangers to be expected from the future, Paganuzzi became ever more authoritarian and inflexible.

The man who acted as mediator between these two tendencies was Professor Giuseppe Toniolo. He was assisted by Mons. Radini-Tedeschi. Despite their active attempts at mediation, the conflict was unhappily re-

solved by the dissolution of the *Opera dei Congressi* at
the beginning of the pontificate of Pius X (1903) who
severely censured the Christian-Democratic trends.

These frequent references to the history of Italian
Catholic Action toward the end of the nineteenth century may appear irrelevant to a biography of John
XXIII. As a matter of fact, however, they are highly
relevant because they allow us to understand the milieu
in which the mind and heart of Don Angelo Roncalli
matured when he became secretary to Mons. Radini-
Tedeschi, who was elected Bishop of Bergamo during
those difficult years.

As the mediator between the two opposing groups,
Mons. Radini-Tedeschi had been as alien to the intransigence of Paganuzzi and his severe Venetian friends as he
was to the generous but often demagogic enthusiasms of
the younger elements. He understood that at bottom
these impulses represented inescapable historical and
spiritual exigencies. The problem was to clarify these
requirements doctrinally and to translate them into pur-
posive and effective action. With respect to his attitude
toward Christian democracy, Mons. Radini-Tedeschi
shared Professor Toniolo's view that it behooved Catholics to attend to the needs of the working classes, to
guard over their interests and to promote their welfare.

Dr. Giacomo Radini-Tedeschi was appointed Bishop
of Bergamo by an apostolic brief of January 20, 1905.
A few days before, in a private audience, Pius X had
said to him: ". . . Monsignore, We thank you for hav-

ing accepted the nomination as Bishop of Bergamo. You had been proposed for Palermo, I said no; they proposed you for Ravenna, I said no. How about Bergamo? And I said yes. Go up there. Bergamo, for those things that can console a bishop, is the first diocese in Italy . . ."

An authoritative lay exponent of Italian Catholicism, Marquis Filippo Crispolti, had written as far back as 1890: "Whenever they are dispirited, Italian Catholics recover their spirits by the thought that in Bergamo all things Catholic succeed. . . ."

Don Angelo Roncalli expressed a similar opinion when in 1916 he published his memoirs of Mons. Giacomo Maria Radini-Tedeschi: "In Bergamo the clergy and laity had been cooperating for thirty years, working with a marvelous success in the very extensive field of Catholic Action. Its authoritative head was Count Medolago, aided by the indefatigable and incomparable apostle Niccolò Rezzara. From that time onward all Italy watched Bergamo. . . ."

There was no mystery about this renaissance. Since 1877, the date of a memorable Catholic Congress held in the Lombard city, yeoman efforts had been made to keep the workers of Bergamo united to Catholicism. At a time when the first signs of socialism—tinged with anarchism—began to make headway among Italian workers, the social aspects and value of the Gospel were being affirmed in that city. Even before the *Rerum Novarum* (1891) of Leo XIII laid down the principle for the work in this direction, Bergamasco Catholics were working effectively among the laboring classes. The fact that they reached the working people earlier and with a better program than the Socialists explains the mystery of this renaissance of Catholic life.

Providentially Mons. Radini knew how to harvest this precious heritage and also how to enrich it by co-ordinating and disciplining the numerous and fresh religious and social forces in the Bergamo diocese. The new bishop was also to carry out far-reaching ecclesiastical reforms, beginning with the administration of the seminary. In 1910 he was to summon the diocesan synod which had not met in Bergamo for many decades, and this synod produced many important decrees. And he also introduced many wise changes in parochial structure and in sacred music, and did much to increase propaganda for the missions.

After his Roman interlude, as we have seen, Don Angelo Roncalli returned to his native region as the secretary of the new Bishop of Bergamo. He remained with him for the entire nine years of his episcopate and found in him not only his spiritual father but a wise and prudent teacher. He accompanied him everywhere and in 1905 went for the first time with him to France and later to Spain and the Holy Land.

There are still some people living in Bergamo who remember Don Angelo Roncalli as he served his bishop in the cathedral or went with him on his visits to the parishes of the city and of the diocese. Others remember him celebrating Mass in the little churches of the upper city which were so dear to him: at San Salvatore, and at

San Michele dell' Arco, where on Sundays he instructed the children in catechism.

A youth, hardly more than a boy, often helped him by serving Mass. His name was Carlo Perico and he was preparing for the priesthood. He was to give proof of the highest qualities of mind and heart in the diplomatic service of the Holy See, and later in the Congregation for the Oriental Church, and Don Angelo was to remain greatly attached to him up to the day of his premature death.

At that time Don Angelo Roncalli's activities were already intensive and widespread. His Spartan habit of not sleeping more than four hours a night goes back to this period of his life. At first this regime had been imposed by necessity, but little by little it became a habit.

The young priest, in fact, was not alone the bishop's secretary. He was most devoted to his pastoral duties and in addition he was a professor at the diocesan seminary. From 1906 to 1912 he taught church history and apologetics, and then patristics. The subject matter of such courses cannot be improvised, so to speak, by an easy-going professor, but require constant and serious preparation. On the other hand, it is known that the teacher perfects himself and his own preparation by the exercise of his ministry. Thus it was with Don Angelo. His pupils of that time still remember the lectures of the young teacher as models of precision and clarity. They also remember the constant warning that came from his lips: "Always be ready to answer those who ask you the reasons for your faith."

Professor Roncalli was not a pedant and he was not

rigidly scholastic. His lectures on the most abstract subjects were alive and interesting, introducing the students to the main currents of modern thought and widening the horizons of their minds. He asked few questions and was very understanding and generous in his judgments, encouraging and revitalizing even the least prepared student. It was enough for him to perceive on the part of the student the slightest interest or awareness of the fundamental problems of the subject matter to heap praise and encouragement on him.

This is how a former student, now Father Cesare Patelli, remembers his old professor Roncalli:

"We would watch him as he came into the class for his lecture, often a little late because of his other duties and sometimes breathing hard because of the many steps in the old seminary; but once in the presence of the students he became at once serene and attentive. Often he brought along notes—the result of hours of sleepless nights—which he would put at the disposal of the students. They were indications, little openings to the greater horizons of our subjects, stimulating us to reading, study and research. Many of his former students owe a passion for study and research which has remained with them throughout their lives—despite the exigencies of their ministry—to the example of this expert teacher."

His teaching activity also developed his own love for historical studies. It was at this time that he began his researches on Cardinal Baronius, the founder of scientific ecclesiastical historiography, as well as studies devoted to the ancient charitable institution of the Misericordia

Maggiore in Bergamo. It was also at this time that he planned and began his basic work on the apostolic visit made by St. Charles Borromeo in 1575 to the territory of Bergamo. The manuscript documents concerning this subject are preserved in 39 large, dusty volumes in the archiepiscopal archives of Milan.

On several occasions Don Angelo had to accompany his bishop to Milan for meetings of the Lombard episcopate. It was precisely at such times that the young priest, so fond of historical research, began to frequent the archiepiscopal archives and the Ambrosian Library. Mons. Achille Ratti, then prefect of the Ambrosiana, took an immediate liking to Don Angelo and encouraged him in his studies. Thus it was that a love of learning led to the encounter between two future Popes.

Don Angelo began to reorganize the documents and to decipher and study them. His was a thorough-going investigation of facts and data of a religious, civil, social and economic character which he wished to interpret and collate in the light of modern experience. This long and tedious research resulted in five published volumes of notable religious, historical and humanistic interest.

Angelo Roncalli also had a particular interest in books, especially rare ones. Any person who knows how to appreciate the beauty and the value of a rare and ancient edition, and the fascination of discovering unknown or forgotten treasures, knows what this means. For him this was a great and abiding interest, and one of which he was to give many evidences later.

Yet during all the years spent in his native region Angelo Roncalli received his most valuable instruction, not from books, but from Bishop Radini-Tedeschi. His was a teaching of piety rooted in a deep inward life and one transmitted more by example than by words. It was a teaching made up of experiences lived and meditated upon during a lifetime spent in doing good for the love of Christ and man.

In October 1916 a great Italian Catholic, whose case for beatification has been introduced, wrote a letter to Don Angelo Roncalli containing an enlightening tribute to Bishop Radini-Tedeschi.

Giuseppe Toniolo, an esteemed professor of economics at the University of Pisa, had known the Bishop of Bergamo very well, and as we know had been associated with him in an effort to solve the differences in the *Opera dei Congressi*. His letter was in acknowledgment of the volume which Mons. Roncalli had written in memory of the deceased Bishop of Bergamo.

"Yesterday I received your commemorative volume on His Excellency Mons. Radini-Tedeschi, the saintly bishop who was the wise, ardent, and balanced initiator and moderator of every form of collective Catholic action, the frank, sure, inflexible espouser of our faith, a faith illumined by science, and made fruitful by an unquenchable love for Jesus in the Blessed Sacrament, for the Immaculate Virgin, the Holy Church, and the Pontificate. . . . I still felt grateful to the Lord for having given this elect soul so felicitous and profound an interpreter and one who makes us understand the nature and the value, even in our time, of the Catholic apostolate in which a renaissance of Christian civilization is being prepared in blood and sorrow. Finally I even felt, and quite rightly, humiliation and almost remorse because I did not profit adequately from the example that he set for so many, and even for me personally, and from his attitude of special friendship toward me and my family. Nor did I make an adequate effort to second, disseminate and translate his teachings in the form of public acts, something which he had expected and hoped for from my humble and fraternal collaboration in the unity of that faith. He was enlightened, industrious and disciplined in the service of that pontificate in which he did so much in a short time, leaving behind fruitful examples of his zeal which I hope will be truly imperishable . . ." [3]

Professor Toniolo added that when the history of the Italian episcopate would be written—something by the way which has yet to be done—the memory of the Bishop of Bergamo would shine like a "morning star" wherever efforts were being made to hasten the victory of Christ.

We have quoted copiously from this letter not only because the person who wrote it may on some not distant tomorrow be the Blessed Giuseppe Toniolo, but also because the writer was one of those Catholics who knew how to serve both his Church and his country. His spiritual sympathy with Bishop Radini-Tedeschi and with his young secretary is not without significance. In fact it shows us to which tendency of Italian Catholicism the future John XXIII belonged.

To explain the connection more fully it is necessary

---

[3] Giuseppe Toniolo, *Lettere*, vol. III, p. 447; *Opera Omnia*, Città del Vaticano, 1953.

to go back a little. Some months before the naming of
Mons. Radini to the episcopal see of Bergamo an event
of great importance for the history of Italian Catholics
took place when the injunctions of the *non expedit*
were relaxed in 1905 and Catholics gradually resumed a
place in the political life of Italy. In Bergamo the first
Catholic deputy, the lawyer Agostino Cameroni, was
elected.

In the elections which followed, in 1909 and then in
1913, a lively controversy was aroused when Catholics
voted for Liberal candidates as long as they offered guar-
antees of a religious character.

At that time Don Luigi Sturzo, the future founder
of the Italian "Partito Popolare" wrote in his newspaper,
La Croce di Costantino: "We must fight the socialists:
but with 'our' forces and 'our' ideas which not only
have a religious value but also one that is social and
democratic. By supporting the conservatives, moreover,
we do the work of reactionaries, in that we go counter
to a complex of aspirations and vital forces which correspond to the needs of the proletariat, and to the future
of Christian social forces. . . ."

During the preparation for the 1913 elections, professor Niccolò Rezzara, president of the diocesan social
action committee sent a memorandum to the head of
the Italian Catholic Electoral Union. One of the signers
was Don Angelo Roncalli. The memorandum pointed
out that in some of the electoral districts of the province
of Bergamo, Catholics should be permitted to vote for
candidates of solid religious principles who were aware
of social problems.

The memorandum displeased the central bodies in Rome who were of the opinion that Rezzara was going too fast and forgetting the prudent directives of the Holy See with respect to political elections. Things seemed to be going badly and Mons. Radini-Tedeschi rushed off to Rome with his faithful secretary Don Angelo Roncalli. He reached there just in time to prevent painful consequences for Rezzara, a profoundly Christian man. On June 28, 1913, he wrote Rezzara: "Undoubtedly there were some who, to the harm of the diocesan administration, tried to prove that this was contrary to pontifical directives. It is something highly painful. But I have not failed to explain and to set things straight. . . ."

Mons. Radini-Tedeschi was a bishop of deep Christian piety. But he was modern without "modernism," so to speak, and responsive to the economic and social needs of the workers without distortions of principle or practice. And he was a tenacious defender of truth and justice—the corollaries of such an attitude—in the spirit of charity.

"There was something of the martial spirit in his soul: a love for a good fight when it was for a good cause, for the Church, the Pope, and for the rights of the people. He disliked to fight with tin swords; if the battle were worth fighting it should be fought with blazing cannon; and as a knight he preferred an open sky and wide fields for his campaigns." [4]

This aspect of the Bishop's character was displayed

---

[4] Angelo Roncalli: *In Memoria di Mons. Giacomo Radini-Tedeschi, Vescovo di Bergamo*, p. 134.

most brilliantly in his struggles for the rights of the common man. It is described by Angelo Roncalli when he writes of the fifty-day strike in Ranica, a town in the province of Bergamo, in 1909:

"When there began the strike in Ranica, about which there was so much publicity, the name of the Bishop appeared among the first and most generous donors to the bread fund of the strikers, even though he had maintained a prudent reserve during the preceding agrarian disturbances.

"Many were scandalized by his action, and less than benevolent information was dispatched to his superiors. Some people, even of good heart, believed that any cause loses its right to support because the use of certain means opens the way to intemperate actions. Mons. Radini did not subscribe to this philosophy. The question in Ranica was not a simple one of wages or of personalities, but one of principle: the fundamental principle of the right of Christian labor to organize against the powerful organization of capital. In that incident, taking the side of the strikers was for him a highly Christian duty, as he himself wrote, and one of justice, of charity, of social peace. He let them scream therefore and calmly continued his keen interest in the cause of the strikers, lamenting, pitying and correcting the inevitable inconvenience to persons and order which are part of a struggle of this nature." [5]

Don Angelo Roncalli could not have had a more lofty and inspired teacher. It was his good fortune to be in close contact with one of the most illustrious and

[5] *Ibid.*, pp. 90 ff.

wisest bishops that Italy has ever had, thereby enlarging his mental horizons and deepening his priestly formation and education.

He was never to forget those years and the memory of Bishop Radini was to remain with him in thousands of circumstances in his conversations, remembrances and prayers. On his desk in Venice the Patriarch kept an old notebook, bound in brown leather with gilt edges, containing the spiritual diary of Mons. Radini-Tedeschi, from which he occasionally read aloud excerpts to visitors. There is no doubt that this notebook is now on the desk of the Pope in the study on the third floor of the Apostolic Palace.

Angelo Roncalli also was to have a special affection for Mons. Radini-Tedeschi's native city, Piacenza. He often went there to visit the Radini family and the various ecclesiastical institutions in the city, in particular the Cristoforo Colombo institute which is the motherhouse of the Pious Society of the Missionaries of St. Charles for Italian emigrants, established by Bishop Scalabrini. One of his last visits was made in 1953, when he went to Piacenza for the episcopal consecration of his collaborator in the Paris nunciature, Mons. Silvio Oddi, now apostolic internuncio to Egypt.

Mons. Radini-Tedeschi was very fond of Don Angelo Roncalli, who had the human misfortune but the priestly consolation of being at his Bishop's bedside when he drew his last breath. The faithful secretary recited the last prayers prescribed by the Church for the consolation of the dying. At a certain point it seemed to Don Angelo that the Bishop had lost consciousness, so he stopped praying. The dying Bishop slowly opened his eyes with great effort and murmured, "Courage, courage, Don Angelo. Continue, I understand everything."

He died on August 22, 1914, two days before the death of St. Pius X. In addition to living in Christ, he lives in the memory and heart of Pope John XXIII.

III

•••••••••••••

The Missionary Vocation

MONS. RADINI-TEDESCHI died on August 22, 1914, when the war was already drenching Europe in blood, and just two days before the death of St. Pius X. And, like his Pope, he died offering his life for peace.

Shortly thereafter, in the spring of 1915, Italy entered the conflict. Don Angelo Roncalli, who had served his obligatory stretch in the army at the age of twenty, was recalled as a private and assigned to the medical corps. Several months later he was promoted to sergeant-major and finally to a chaplaincy with the rank of lieutenant. He himself described the spirit with which he performed his duty in the preface of the book he wrote in 1916, dedicated to the memory of Bishop Radini-Tedeschi.

"These pages were written while war raged in Europe, the terrible war that has cost so much blood and tears. And they were written and collected not in the quiet of a study but during the performance of the most varied tasks by one who, following the example and the teachings of Bishop Radini, gave the best he could to his country at the hour of its supreme trial; at first as a common soldier, then in the lower non-commissioned ranks of the army, and then more directly as a priest. His intention was to contribute, no matter how humbly, to rendering his country truly and greatly loved, free and great in the light of Christ by ministering to the spiritual relief and comfort of her valiant soldiers."

Angelo Roncalli belonged to that group of Italian Catholics, clerical and lay, whose thoughts and hopes were that the blood sacrifices of the war would not be made in vain; but that in expiation of evil they would contribute to the uplift of the Italian conscience and the spiritual betterment of their country. What conclusions did he draw from the experience? He himself tells us in a letter he sent to the President of the Association of Italian Chaplains in 1956:

"I am grateful to the Lord . . . but I particularly thank Him because it was His wish that I perform my military service at the age of twenty, and that I should serve again later as a sergeant and chaplain. How great the knowledge of the human heart this affords! How great the grace of experience I received in dedication, sacrifice, and in the understanding of life and the priestly apostolate!"

Following Italy's entry into the war, Don Angelo Roncalli spent his days in the Clementina and Porta Nuova military hospitals in Bergamo at the bedside of the wounded, who arrived continuously from the front in long, sorrowful convoys. He showed a great understanding for all the miseries of the body and spirit, and this understanding enabled him to lift the fallen, support the weak and strengthen even the strong who, shaken by the drama of life at the front, questioned the reason for so much pain, blood and sorrow. Serene and trustful, he went from one bed to another and infused his own faith in God into the souls of the wounded. Providence had endowed Angelo Roncalli with the gift of inspiring human sympathy at first sight. And aware as he was of this natural gift, he used it in the service of God and His cause.

At the time of the election of John XXIII no one recalled that as a chaplain Don Angelo Roncalli had also served on the fields of battle, in addition to his tours of duty in the military hospitals. The Pope himself filled in this lacuna in his life history when on November 26, 1958, he addressed a British delegation which had come to Italy in connection with the care of British military cemeteries:

"Your presence evokes memories already distant and which remain among the most moving of an already long life. You remind me of the plateau of Asiago and the blood-soaked fields of the Piave, dear to Us because they contain many graves of your valiant dead. We became familiar with these fields during the [first] world war and our period of service as a military chaplain. How many were the wounded We succoured, to how many dying soldiers did We bring the last consolations of friendship and the reconciliation of final absolution, how many graves We blessed surrounded by the comrades-in-arms of the soldier fallen on the field of honor! The chaplain's is a deeply human and brotherly minis-

try in which, in the midst of combatants, the priest remains the witness to the highest moral and religious
values for which those valiant men do not hesitate to
give their lives."

Toward the end of the war came the great epidemic
of "Spanish" influenza to add to the evils and hardships of the times. The chaplain-lieutenant, who combined his ministry of the wounded with his duties as a
professor at the Bergamo seminary, unalterably maintained his personal faith in God. The epidemic struck at
those who had been spared the fire and steel of the
front, and death also took its toll among those who, re-
covering from their wounds, had begun again to look
life hopefully in the face. In his tour of the hospitals
Don Angelo was always ready to assist and comfort the
double victims of the war and the epidemic.

But even the storm of this disaster passed away. The
armistice was declared and in 1918 Don Angelo was
freed of his military commitments for good.

In the days immediately following the election of
John XXIII, Dr. Giuseppe Fumagalli recalled the time
when he was paymaster of the military district of Bergamo. He tells the following story of the day in 1918
when Don Angelo Roncalli presented himself to him in
order to collect his discharge bonus:

"As I was processing his service record for the final
payment the future Pope spoke to me of his impressions
of military life and he made the following declaration
which I have never forgotten: 'There is a great comfort
in the discipline that makes everybody equal in the

presence of duty and which gives so much dignity and comfort to one who does his work zealously, by offering the hardships and sacrifices that it involves to the Lord.' After finishing my computations I handed him the sum owed him after four years of service. It was not very much, although I do not remember the exact figure. I would say, however, that it didn't even come to a thousand lire. As he pocketed that paltry sum, he added: 'Look, it's not much, but still it's precious to me because I can use it to meet the expenses I am incurring in order to open a students' house in Bergamo.' "

In the heart of the oldest quarter in Bergamo, on Via San Salvatore, there stands a patrician house known as the Palazzo Asperti which has lost nothing of its dignity with the passage of time. Persons entering from the street come upon a little courtyard encircled by porticos and by colonnaded porches on the first and second stories. At the end of the first landing of the main staircase hangs a huge and handsome mirror, somewhat darkened by time but still in good condition, beneath which is the legend: *Nosce Te Ipsum*—"Know Thyself."

The building became the property of the diocese of Bergamo around 1915; the availability of ample and suitable quarters in the vicinity of secondary schools had immediately inspired Don Angelo Roncalli with the idea of establishing a boarding house and club for students. At that time—and to a certain extent this is still true—the smaller Italian cities did not have any advanced secondary schools. Once they graduated from their local *ginnasie* (or high schools), students who wanted to continue their studies had to leave their homes and attend classes in the higher institutions of learning to be found in the nearest big city. Unless they happened to be the guests of relatives or friends, they lived alone in furnished rooms, away from the affectionate vigilance of their family at the very time they were undergoing all the strains and stresses of beginning maturity.

This was then the situation in Bergamo. The so-called upper section of the city contained a classical lyceum, a Normal School, and an Accountants' Institute. Naturally this section of the city also contained a vast, exuberant and fun-loving student population. For quite some time now Don Angelo had occupied himself with the affairs and problems of youth. During the entire period that he served as Bishop Radini's secretary, he was also, as we have seen, a beloved and admired professor at the diocesan seminary. Even then he had actively promoted Catholic Action groups among young people, and he continued to teach at the seminary even after the death of his bishop.

After the war Don Angelo could at last realize the project he had planned to solve the problem of the student youth, and open to them the beautiful and spacious quarters at the Palazzo Asperti. Thus the first "Casa dello Studente" (student house) to be established in Italy came into being in this ancient and noble structure. It contained a chapel, rooms for male students, study and recreation rooms. Nearby was also the student branch of Catholic Action, "Sant' Alessandro," where the young people of Bergamo could meet with out-of-town students in order to educate themselves in an openly Christian spirit and dedicate themselves to apostolic activities in the surrounding neighborhoods.

Many people who were young at that time, and whose hair—if they have any—is now gray or white, and who now may even be deputies in the Italian Parliament and undersecretaries of State, were frequent visitors in these halls and assemblies. With deep appreciation they recall the tireless apostolate of Don Angelo Roncalli who was among his young people during all the hours left him from his teaching, his favorite studies, and his always exemplary priestly ministry.

Here in the rooms whose walls were adorned with damask tapestries, he would encourage the youths, aid them in their studies, discreetly see them through minor financial crises, help them plan house programs, and above all support them during the trials and disturbances of adolescence. The principal salon, decorated in yellow tones and adorned with a painting depicting the death of the poet Tasso, still looks as it did forty years ago, and still echoes to the talks, devoid of professorial airs or mannerisms, that Don Angelo used to make to his young friends.

An orderly person himself, Don Angelo was of the view that spiritual order should correspond with outer order, and that neatness was a tangible sign of self-respect. The mirror on the first landing of the staircase had been placed there at his suggestion. The reflected image and the Latin inscription, "Know thyself" repeating the injunction of the ancient sage, were a silent warning to the boys as they were about to leave the house.

Don Roncalli, as founder and director of the student house as well as spiritual adviser to the student Catholic Action group, "Sant' Alessandro," lived in the Palazzo Asperti. From the windows of his apartment he could see the ancient walls of the convent of Santa Grata *"in Columnellis."* The memory of this former residence must have come back to his mind when as nuncio in Paris he discovered an ancient codex which turned out to be a collection of sacred hymns, beautifully painted with miniatures, and written in the fourteenth century for the nuns of Santa Grata. This convent is one of the oldest in Northern Italy and here the Saint's remains have been venerated since 1027.

Seventeen years of Don Roncalli's priesthood in Bergamo were marked by a lively and daily participation in numerous activities and projects of the Bergamesco Catholic Action group among all levels of the population: Christian doctrine classes for high school students; cultural talks at the evening schools; religious moderator of the Union of Catholic Women; the founding of the first young Catholic women's associations in the city and diocese.

At the same time that he was devoting so much effort to the fatherly care of the students, he was carrying on an equally intense activity at the diocesan seminary, one to which he was committed in a still larger sense. The seminary had reopened after its forced closing during the war when the young seminarians had been called up

for military service. Some of them died on the battlefield and some, though they survived the war, did not
return. And many of those who did resume their interrupted studies had undergone shattering experiences in
a world the reality of which was quite different from
the one they had imagined. Often these youths were
disturbed and disoriented.

Bishop Marelli, successor to Mons. Radini-Tedeschi,
felt the gravity of the moral and spiritual problems that
assailed his seminarians, and understood the indispensable need for a spiritual director who was experienced in
life and fully aware of its crude realities, as well as one
who was open-minded and of a paternal disposition.
Thus the bishop urged Don Angelo Roncalli, who was
then teaching apologetics and patristics at the seminary,
to give up his courses and become the spiritual director
of the seminary. So during the last three years of his
stay in Bergamo Don Angelo conducted this extremely
delicate activity of the priestly apostolate along with
the assiduous labors which he devoted to the student
population of Bergamo. That it was an activity crowned
by the most flattering success is attested to by the worthy priests and prelates, now elevated to high ecclesiastical posts, who were once his spiritual sons.

The rooms of the Palazzo Asperti have remained almost unchanged, even though more mature tenants have
taken the place of the students of former times. The
higher institutions of learning are no longer in "upper"
Bergamo but have been moved to newer sections in the
lower city. The peace and quiet of the old quarter is no
longer enlivened by the exuberant animation of student

youth, and for this reason a visitor who returns to the old places gets the impression that time has come to a stop.

Don Angelo Roncalli imbued the activity of the Palazzo Asperti with his priestly zeal, combined with a missionary spirit. In fact, a love for the missions had been alive in him for a long time. It had borne him up on his tours of the hospitals during the war, and now it accompanied him as the spiritual director of the diocesan seminary, driving him to efforts to deepen the sense of Christ in his fellows, especially among the youth; to render this spirit active in day-to-day life, to infuse it with gentleness and simplicity in those places where it was ignored or misunderstood.

Here we should quote Don Angelo Roncalli himself on the theory that an accurate biography must base itself where possible on direct evidence. On March 3, 1958, Cardinal Roncalli, the Patriarch of Venice, went to Milan and, at the headquarters of the Pontifical Institute of Foreign Missions, delivered an address in which he said:

". . . I remember the first time that Providence led me to the Pontifical Institute of Foreign Missions on Via Monterosa in Milan, in the autumn of 1910, a half century ago. I had come as the young secretary of my great teacher and master, Mons. Radini-Tedeschi, on the occasion of the presentation of the cross to a wonderful group of departing missionaries. In confidential talks with some of the older missionaries who had just returned from the mission fields . . . I was seized by a feeling of edification, by an indescribable affection which was not yet strong enough to awaken a frank and courageous missionary vocation in me, but educated my spirit to a deep admiration for, and a lively interest in, those who had heard this call and had responded by embarking on that bold and mysterious road."

He did not then have the heart to leave Bergamo: he was too attached to his bishop and perhaps he thought that even without leaving the country a fruitful apostolate was possible. But the missionary desire had awakened in him and his love for the missions in distant lands was solidly confirmed.

In that same year, 1910, the Missionary Union of the Clergy was established in Italy and Don Angelo was among the first to apply for membership in this confraternity of priests which establishes a spiritual bridge between the vanguards of the Church who are bringing Christ to lands where He is still the great Unknown, and other priests who work in a different kind of mission in order to maintain and consolidate the reign of God in souls already Christian.

In 1920 the National Eucharistic Congress was held in Bergamo. On that occasion Don Angelo made a memorable speech on "The Eucharist and Our Lady." Several cardinals and many high prelates of the Curia, bishops, clergy and thousands of faithful were present. Was it this speech that made Mons. Radini's former secretary known beyond the city's circles? Or, instead, did someone bring him to the attention of his ecclesiastical superiors?

Nobody knows the answers to these questions. One thing that is certain is that Pope Benedict XV, who had been a devoted friend of Mons. Radini, knew Don Angelo Roncalli very well. So when someone mentioned him as a possible choice for the directorship of the Society for the Propagation of the Faith in Italy, the Pope gladly acted upon this suggestion. Thus it was that Mons. Roncalli, who in the meantime had been nominated honorary canon of Bergamo and domestic prelate of His Holiness, left his city and returned to Rome from which he had departed seventeen years before as a young priest to follow his "teacher and master."

Mons. Roncalli was to spend four years in the ancient and majestic building of the Propaganda Fide on Piazza di Spagna; four years marked by intensive, laborious and productive activity.

His departure from Bergamo marked a decisive turn in his life. His new duties now took him far beyond the diocesan circle of his activities and interests. Now he had to travel up and down Italy, visiting all the dioceses, in order to organize a stage of cooperation with missionary activity that, following the end of the war, had just been begun under the inspiration of Benedict XV. There were unmistakable signs that sooner or later the colonial peoples would become independent, and it was felt that it was necessary for the Church to expand and win support for her worldwide missionary effort, disassociated from the political interests of any one nation.

Don Angelo was in Rome in 1922 when Pope Benedict died after a brief but glorious pontificate. One of the first acts of his successor Pius XI was to transfer the central committee of the Society for the Propagation of the Faith from Lyons, France, to Rome and to coordinate its activities under the direction of the Pope and the Congregation of the Propaganda.

In the first two years of his activity Mons. Roncalli reorganized the work of the Society in Italy, unifying the diverse regional centers and establishing a National Council of which he was the first president. In this capacity, and later as a member of the Higher Council of the international Society, he had to take part in the organization of congresses and the maintenance of contacts with other national organizations. In establishing new regulations for missionary cooperation with his colleagues in other countries, the spirit of the founder—the Frenchwoman Pauline Jaricot—was always respected but adapted to the exigencies of the new times.

Therefore he had to travel a great deal abroad. He visited Paris, Lyons, Brussels, Aachen, Vienna, Munich, and many other European cities. At his initiative and under his direction the Italian review, *"The Propagation of the Faith in the World"* was founded in 1923. Soon the publication achieved a circulation of 100,000 copies, a respectable figure in itself, but quite impressive in a country like Italy. The many articles written by Don Angelo during the first two years of the periodical's existence abundantly prove that for him his missionary labors were a true apostolate and not just a bureaucratic task.

But these preoccupations did not lead him to abandon or neglect his ministry as a priest. He continued to hear confessions and to hold spiritual exercises for laymen and clergy, and he also taught religion to young people. In 1925 he returned to the Roman Seminary which he had left after his ordination as a priest in 1905. The seminary was no longer at the old address but had moved to the new building which Pius X had built near the basilica of St. John in the Lateran. This time he returned as a professor and taught patristics for a few months.

The Pope himself recalled these lectures on the occasion of his recent visit to the Pontifical Lateran Athenaeum, November 28, 1958:

"He who now speaks to you was one day invited by the Most Eminent Cardinal Vicar of His Holiness, Basilio Pompili—who does not remember him with respectful sympathy?—to take the place, here in the Lateran, of a professor of patristics who had just died.

"We gave only fifteen lectures, because almost immediately there arrived an order to leave the movement of missionary cooperation and to leave Rome for the Near East.

"Those fifteen lectures, from the apostolic Fathers to St. Cyprian, were of such lively interest to Us that even now, at a distance of thirty-three years, we find in them cause of humble but sincere exaltation. We do not know to what our success was due; but we do remember well the attention and the applause with which our beloved students of that time followed and underlined every lecture, and their surprise at the unexpected termination of those lectures. . . .

"Permit me with the utmost humility to express the hope that during the next academic year all your lectures will manage to bring that same sense of satisfaction and happiness, both in the teaching of the professors and the attention of the students."

In 1924, ten years after his death, the mortal remains of Mons. Radini-Tedeschi were exhumed from the city cemetery of Bergamo to be transferred to the bishop's crypt in the cathedral. Don Angelo Roncalli had already been for three years at the Propaganda Fide in Rome, but he returned to Bergamo in order to be present for the final honors and tributes accorded to his spiritual father and teacher. A solemn funeral service was celebrated on April 29 in the cathedral in the presence of the civic authorities and a great number of people. Toward the end of the rites the former faithful secretary of Mons. Radini-Tedeschi made a memorial address for his bishop at the moment when the remains were about to be placed alongside those of the other bishops of the diocese of Bergamo. He said:

"As this very sad gathering comes to a close, the heart nonetheless experiences the gentle solace that comes from a finished task well done. Courage, therefore, brethren, and let us go forward, let us go forward all together along the path of peace: in *viam pacis*. Let us be guided by the last words which that true great servant of God and the Church whom we have just honored addressed to us in his last testament: 'I commend justice, truth and charity to all.' May the invocation 'Peace, for Peace' that came from his dying lips and which was to be his final word be also ours."

Pope Pius XI had known Mons. Radini-Tedeschi very well. On June 4, 1893, the bishop as papal ablegate had delivered to President Sadi Carnot two cardinals' hats which Leo XIII sent to the French prelates Lecot and Bourret. He was accompanied by a secretary who was none other than Don Achille Ratti.

The Pope therefore knew Don Angelo Roncalli as the product of an excellent teacher. He had met him about twenty years before in the Ambrosian Library and had followed his extensive activities with the Society for the Propagation of the Faith. When, in the Jubilee Year of 1925, Pope Pius thought the time had come to send an apostolic visitor to Bulgaria, he was particularly reminded of Don Angelo and named him titular archbishop, entrusting him with the Bulgarian mission.

According to Mons. Roncalli the Pope "had transferred to him the friendship he felt for the deceased Bishop Radini." Among other things they shared in common their love of the great nineteenth-century novelist Alessandro Manzoni. Both were indefatigable readers of *I Promessi Sposi*, and Mons. Roncalli often cited passages of incidents from this Italian classic in his conversations, sermons or writings.

Mons. Angelo Giuseppe Roncalli was elevated to the titular see of Areopoli and consecrated archbishop in Rome in the Church of San Carlo al Corso on March 19, 1925, by Cardinal Tacci, secretary of the Sacred Congregation for the Oriental Church. He was assisted by Bishop Marchetti Selvaggiani, Secretary of the Congregation for the Propagation of the Faith, and by the Vicar-General of Rome, Mons. Palica. The new archbishop's first Mass was celebrated on the tomb of St. Peter.

For the consecration of their son, Giovanni and Barianna Roncalli made their first trip to Rome. Their cup was filled when after the ceremony they were received in audience by Pope Pius XI, who blessed them and said he shared their joy at seeing their son an archbishop.

Immediately after his consecration Mons. Roncalli made a quick journey to Bergamo where a solemn academic gathering in his honor was held at the seminary. Then he left for his new post. He had been consecrated on the feast day of St. Joseph; by March 25 he was already in Sofia ready to begin his new work. He was faced with a difficult task. Although apostolic visitors have no diplomatic status, they must often meet with civil authorities and negotiate questions concerning Catholics with them. Civil authorities, moreover, are inclined to view them as Vatican envoys. Mons. Roncalli had to prepare himself for his new task when he was already head over heels in work. But, being calm and serene by nature, he was not at a loss, just as he was never to be at a loss for any reason.

At 6:30 on the morning following his election, John XXIII telephoned Count Dalla Torre, director of the *Osservatore Romano*, who hastily slipped on his formal morning coat and hastened to the apartment of the Cardinal Secretary of State where the Pope had spent the night. The Count, who is an old friend of Angelo Giuseppe Roncalli, immediately asked him if he had slept well.

"Why? Shouldn't I have slept well?" replied John XXIII. "I have entrusted myself to the Lord and I have rested as usual."

The new Pope, serene and trustful in God, has always slept tranquilly with no terrors before the arduous tasks which Providence has placed in his path.

It is not surprising then that the Archbishop of Areopoli felt no trepidation at his mission to Sofia.

IV

······················

The Middle East

Apostolic Visitor and Apostolic Delegate

THE MISSION entrusted to Mons. Roncalli was difficult and delicate, requiring pastoral zeal united to human understanding, tolerance and diplomatic tact. There were at that time less than 50,000 Catholics in Bulgaria, divided between the Roman, Byzantine and Armenian rites—a small minority compared with the more than five million members of the Orthodox Church. But in Sofia and several other cities and towns throughout the nation the Catholics were influential and there were some very important schools in the country conducted by French Augustinians of the Assumption, and by several Italian congregations. These centers of study exercised a notable influence even beyond the Catholic community since many Orthodox dissidents sent their sons to the schools of the missionaries.

For historic reasons the religious situation in the country was of an involved nature. Evangelized in the ninth century when one of its czars, Boris (852–888), received baptism and imposed it on his warriors, Bulgaria was for many centuries both politically and religiously in the orbit of Constantinople. It is true that as early as 972 the Holy See had established a metropolitan see at Ochrida and appointed an archbishop with the title of patriarch, but in the seventeenth century this patriarchate was absorbed by the Greek Church and finally suppressed entirely in 1767 by the Phanar, or Greek Patriarch of Constantinople.

When in the middle of the nineteenth century the Bulgarians claimed religious independence from the Phanar, an influential minority declared themselves Catholic. Their act was confirmed by Pius IX on January 21, 1861, and several months later he himself consecrated the first Catholic archbishop of the Eastern rite in modern times in Bulgaria. But the movement toward Rome came to a halt because of its political character and the intervention of Russia. In 1870 the Sultan * authorized the constitution of an autonomous Bulgarian hierarchy, and an Orthodox Bulgarian exarchate came into being two years later when Bishop Hilarion, head of the anti-Phanar party was elected as exarch, an election which the Patriarch of Constantinople refused to recognize and countered by excommunicating the Bulgarians. The national Church of Bulgaria was to continue under its own Orthodox leaders.

However in 1908 Prince Ferdinand of Saxe-Coburg-Gotha took advantage of the revolution in Turkey to declare Bulgaria politically independent with himself

* Bulgaria was subject to Turkey from the 13th to the 19th centuries.

as czar. There was a time on the eve of the Balkan War (1912–1913) when Czar Ferdinand thought of orienting the national Church toward Rome, and even started negotiations in that direction which were interrupted in 1914 by World War I.

At the time of Archbishop Roncalli's appointment as apostolic visitor, there existed a special problem in connection with Catholic missionary action in Bulgaria. On this subject we shall cite what was being written at that time in Italy, with the best intentions in the world but with an obvious misunderstanding of the religious situation in Bulgaria:

"In the post-war period Italy energetically allied herself with France in an effort to control all welfare activities which moreover were entrusted to teaching and nursing religious congregations. Italy consolidated her influence in Bulgaria even through the bond of kinship between the two reigning dynasties. This influence was concretely manifested in the development of Italian schools and especially of an institute which aims to assert things Italian and Catholic in that Danubian country: I refer to the Society Pro Oriente of Father Galloni which for some time has controlled all the Italian scholastic and welfare institutions in Bulgaria." [1]

All this was in contradiction to the wishes of the Holy See which Benedict XV had made known by word and deed in the immediate post-war period, and which has later been confirmed by his successor. Religion had to be freed from any political servitude and it was clear that in Bulgaria rival foreign powers sought to exploit

[1] Mario Bendiscioli, *La Politica della Santa Sede;* Florence, 1939, p. 149.

religious feelings for their own purposes, certainly against the will of the missionaries themselves.

This was the situation when Mons. Angelo Giuseppe Roncalli was nominated apostolic visitor. Anyone aware of the facts did not have to ponder for long in order to understand the purpose behind his mission. It was a question of releasing Catholics and the missionary institutions from any commitments of a political character, and at the same time of making contact with the larger religious group in the country, to sound out its spirit and disposition toward Rome.

However, it would be a grave mistake to assert that the apostolic visitor had been sent to Sofia with the task of restoring unity between Rome and the dissident Bulgarian Church. Yet the presence of an apostolic visitor, fully justified and indeed made necessary by the imperative requirements of the Catholic community, would eventually permit direct contacts with the Orthodox hierarchy and a deeper knowledge of the general religious problems of Bulgaria.

Before appointing Mons. Roncalli Pius XI had received a report on the religious situation in Bulgaria from a priest of the Oriental rite named Cyril Korolevskij, who was and still is an authority on the Eastern world and a most competent bibliophile. Soon after his election Pius XI, who never forgot that he himself had been a librarian, had sent two Vatican "writers" to the Orient: Father Cyril and a French prelate named Mons. Eugene Tisserant. Their mission was to look for Eastern codices and books. After a long stay in Bulgaria Father Korolevskij, an acute and intelligent observer, wrote a report and sent it to Pius XI. In the farewell audience which Pius XI granted to Mons. Roncalli before his departure for Bulgaria he suggested that this report be read and studied very carefully.

On the evening of his election John XXIII remembered Father Cyril, who is now an octogenarian and in frail health but still alert mentally. On receiving Cardinal Tisserant's homage he asked about the priest and on learning that he was still alive the Holy Father asked the Cardinal to take Father Cyril his first apostolic blessing. This Cardinal Tisserant did on the following day, paying a visit to his old friend in his modest Roman dwelling.

Mons. Roncalli began his mission by first fulfilling his pastoral duties; he cared for his flock, visited everyone and went everywhere and rapidly learned the language of the country, remembering always that to the Bulgarians he was a foreigner and must not offend the national sensibilities.

There is an episode which reveals not only the harmony of his relationships but the affectionate familiarity that existed between the apostolic visitor to Bulgaria and Pius XI. During a visit to Rome Mons. Roncalli spoke to the Pope about a dissident Bulgarian bishop with whom he had become very friendly. In their talks the Bulgarian prelate had declared that he could not understand how the jurisdictional primacy of the Roman See over the Churches could be denied. Links of various kinds, however, prevented the bishop from accepting the logical consequences of this conviction.

The Pope listened with great interest and agreed with Mons. Roncalli's suggestion that he give the "dissident Catholic" something to remember him by. He opened his desk drawer and took out some holy cards which he handed to Mons. Roncalli. The latter looked at the Pope without saying a word, but he made the Pontiff understand that this gift was a trifle too modest.

"Too little you think?" asked Pius XI smiling. Then he rummaged through his desk drawer again and came up with a gold medal engraved with his portrait.

Mons. Roncalli brought this tangible memento of the Pope to the Orthodox bishop who had it mounted in gold and who wore it around his neck, as is the custom among Eastern bishops, along with his regular pectoral cross. According to Mons. Roncalli, the medal from the Pope hung around the neck of the prelate as he lay in state after his death.

From such incidents as this we will understand how the new Apostolic Visitor to Bulgaria managed to win universal esteem and affection. His enlightened work and cordial character, always pervaded by a pastoral spirit, had also a deep effect on the small Catholic groups of Bulgaria, and in 1931 his mission was raised by Rome to the rank of an Apostolic Delegation.

An important episode of his mission was connected with the marriage of King Boris of Bulgaria and the events that followed. Princess Giovanna, a daughter of the King of Italy and a devout Catholic, married King Boris in the Church of St. Francis of Assisi in October 1930, after having obtained a papal dispensation making possible a marriage between persons of different religious faiths. The Pope had granted the dispensation on the basis of the usual conditions prescribed by canon law, according to which the children of such a union must be baptized and educated as Catholics. The King had formally committed himself in writing to respect this condition, but the marriage ceremony was repeated in Sofia according to the Orthodox rite and when, in January 1933, the first child was born, the little princess was baptized by the dissident metropolitan Stephan. It was the duty of the Apostolic Delegate, even though he had no diplomatic status, to lodge a protest with the government against the violation of the commitments previously assumed.[2]

Mons. Roncalli rose to the occasion by combining tact with the vigorous reaction called for by this serious incident, and also by showing a particular understanding for the young Czarina, whose will had been ignored. But the episode revealed a state of mind in the dissident Bulgarian Church that could hardly be called well disposed toward Rome. Even though Mons. Roncalli's personal contacts had overcome much of the centuries-old mistrust, the spirit of partisanship still prevailed.

In Bulgaria as apostolic delegate until the end of 1934, Mons. Roncalli cleared up the confused situation which had arisen because of the interference of foreign governments with missionary activities. During his stay in Sofia and that of the papal representatives who were his successors, the small but vital Bulgarian Catholic community was further united; religious life was intensified,

[2] *Documentation Catholique*, tome xxix, col. 209–212. See also *Osservatore Romano*, Jan. 18 and 19, 1933.

and useful programs of Catholic Action initiated. When the Soviet troops entered Sofia in 1944, there were around 57,000 Catholics in a population of 6,078,000 inhabitants. Most of this has now been swept away, as we know, by ten years of savage Communist persecution.

King Boris had died mysteriously a year before the Russian occupation. On November 4, 1958, while the coronation Mass for John XXIII was being celebrated in the Basilica of St. Peter's, a woman wept silently in one of the tribunes. She was Giovanna of Savoy, former Czarina of Bulgaria, now a widow in exile.

Mons. Angelo Roncalli took leave of the Bulgarians in an address delivered on Christmas Day in 1934 in the church of the Capuchin Fathers in Sofia. His talk, broadcast over the radio, was the heartfelt farewell of a friend who departs with a fund of memories that nothing can destroy:

". . . Leaving for the new destination to which I have been assigned, I carry with me a precious remembrance of Bulgaria. I have requested the Holy Father to change my titular archbishopric to that of a marvelous place, the veritable gem of Bulgaria. Henceforth I shall no longer bear the title of archbishop of Areopoli but of archbishop of Mesembria. Thus each day I shall be reminded of Bulgaria, a remembrance that will echo in my heart each time I raise my hand to bless the people on solemn occasions, and every time I hold out my hand to sign a document. And you, beloved brethren, do not forget me, do not forget one who wishes to remain your friend forever, an eternal and zealous friend of Bulgaria.

"According to a tradition preserved up to our day in Catholic Ireland, on Christmas night each family places a light in the window in order to let Joseph and Mary, who might be passing by in search of a refuge, know that inside the house there is a family awaiting them around the fireplace and a table blessed with the gifts of God.

"Dear brethren, no one knows the ways of the future! Wherever I may go in the world, anyone from Bulgaria who might be in distress and who comes by my house at night will find a light in my window. Knock, just knock, and I shall not ask you whether you be Catholic or Orthodox, just knock and enter, brother Bulgarians! You will be received with open arms, and a friendly heart will go out to greet you. For such have been the proofs of charity in the Lord which have made sweet my life during my ten years in Bulgaria . . ."

Even after his departure the memory of Mons. Roncalli remained vivid in the minds of the Bulgarians. Shortly after he left, at the beginning of winter, the new apostolic delegate was anxiously awaiting two car-loads of coal that were supposed to come from Czechoslovakia. Notice of the freight cars' arrival did come, though no one knew where they were exactly. So Don Angelo Prinetto, the young secretary of the Delegation, was assigned the task of looking for the coal. In vain he visited all the railroad yards in and around Sofia; no one had ever even heard of the Apostolic Delegation.

After two or three days of futile search the young Piedmontese priest finally entered a workers' shack in one of the railyards to be greeted by the same answers. However, when Don Prinetto casually mentioned Vi Ulicka number 2, the address of Mons. Roncalli, at the name "Gospodin Roncalli" the faces of the workers brightened. "Big-hearted man, good friend!" they said. Not only were the freight cars quickly found on a dead-end track but the workers organized a caravan of trucks and cars and delivered the coal to the Delegation, even refusing to accept a tip for their services.

Something similar happened a little later at the customs office. The Delegation had been informed that it must pay certain retroactive duties together with penalties. This seemed strange since Mons. Roncalli had received formal exemption from the payment of all customs from King Boris himself. Don Prinetto resumed his pilgrimage through the maze of Bulgarian bureaucracy in order to clear up the mystery. Again none of the offices he visited knew anything of the matter until finally the young secretary, almost speaking to himself, remarked, "And yet Monsignor Roncalli. . . ." Again there was a shout of sudden understanding, "Gospodin Roncalli? Big-hearted man. . . ." After that the exemption declaration, signed by King Boris, was immediately turned up in the files under Monsignor Roncalli's name.

Thus as an ambassador of charity and friendship Angelo Giuseppe Roncalli had entered the hearts of the Bulgarian people and had made familiar the Pope of

Rome and his generosity in a country which hitherto had known little about them.

In Istanbul, on May 16, 1937, a solemn Mass was celebrated in the Latin Cathedral of the Holy Ghost in the presence of the entire Catholic clergy of Turkey. To the amazement of the congregation the officiating archbishop read the Gospel of the day in the Turkish language. This prelate was Monsignor Angelo Giuseppe Roncalli. Transferred three years before to the titular archbishopric of Mesembria, on November 30, 1934, he had been appointed by Pius XI as apostolic delegate to Greece and Turkey and as administrator of the Latin Rite Vicariate of Istanbul.

Here he could act as the priest it was always his great desire to be. There were only a few Catholics in ancient Constantinople and they lived in a hostile environment. Mons. Roncalli could take care of each one of them, so to speak, personally. He would visit churches and religious communities without advance announcement, and he dedicated his care above all to the St. Louis Inter-Ritual Seminary directed by French Capuchins of the province of Paris. During Lent he personally taught catechism to the children.

Following his election as John XXIII, his mission was thus recalled by the Turkish newspaper *Aksam:*

". . . During the years spent in Turkey Mons. Roncalli learned Turkish and made many friends among political figures and the people. One of his most intimate friends was the late Naman Menemengioglu (a former ambassador to Paris). Roncalli had a deep admiration for Ataturk.[3] A friend of the Turks, for the first time in the history of Catholicism he had some prayers translated into Turkish to be recited in the churches of Istanbul."

The Apostolic Delegate had further arranged that the Divine Praises (Blessed be God, etc.), recited immediately after the Mass, be said in Turkish. Such measures taken by Mons. Roncalli corresponded with his great desire to obtain a deeper and more direct participation of the faithful in the celebration of the liturgy. But they were also inspired by considerations of another character.

The mission which Pius XI had entrusted to his friend Don Angelo in 1934 was neither easy nor comfortable. In any case, it appeared to be much more arduous than the one he had carried out in Bulgaria. To a stranger to the Catholic Church it might seem that such work is of slight importance, and that a sojourn in an incomparably beautiful city like Istanbul on the Bosporus, or in Athens in the shadow of the Parthenon, is a kind of diplomatic vacation granted as a reward to deserving prelates or to those in need of a rest. The truth, instead, is quite different.

The modern Turkey of Kemal Ataturk professed to be a secular state, that is, "neutral." As a matter of fact, however, in its relations with religious minorities within the country it was behaving like the old Turkey of the sultans. The process of the destruction of Christianity there had begun with the invasion of the Seljuks in the eleventh century, and can be said to have continued

[3] President of the Turkish Republic who died in 1938.

without interruption until 1923. But before World War II there were still 1,800,000 dissident Greek Orthodox Christians in Asia Minor (with 40 dioceses) and an equal number of Armenians (with 46 dioceses). There were in addition about 130 Christian schools (30 in Istanbul, 21 in Smyrna, 81 in the rest of Asia Minor). In part they were in the hands of non-Catholic Christians, but in the main the schools were Catholic and they exercised a notable influence even among Moslems. It is said, for example, that Ataturk himself attended a French school for a time when he was a boy.

Statistics gathered in 1927 indicated that there were 258,000 Christians in Turkey amid a Moslem population numbering 13½ millions. A total of 179,000 Christians lived in the vicariate of Istanbul, of whom 20,000 were Catholics of the Latin rite; smaller groups of Catholics of the Eastern rites were spread throughout Turkey. These figures were further reduced and there are no figures relative to the Orthodox dissidents. But around 1940 there were no more than 12,000 Catholics (9,000 of the Latin rite and 3,000 of the Byzantine rite). In 1943 the figure was even lower.

This is hardly the place to discuss the great tragedy of the massacres that occurred between 1918 and 1923. It is enough to recall that in the new Turkey the atavistic hatred of the Moslem masses against the "infidel" Christians was allied to the nationalist spirit of the secular regime of Kemal Ataturk.

This regime, as such, was not hostile to religion; it was merely indifferent. Its adherents, at least thirty years ago, despised believers, not out of anti-religious

hatred as is the case with communists, but because
Kemal Ataturk was at one time supposed to have said:
"He who prays is a coward or in every case a useless
being." To the common mentality, shared alike by the
old and new Turks, everything which was Christian
was alien to Turkey. For instance in 1928 when some
women students of the American Protestant school of
Brussa became Christians, the press accused them not
of having abandoned Islam, but of having deliberately
renounced participation in the national community.
Many Christian and Catholic schools were closed for this
very reason, even though the constitution guaranteed
academic freedom within the framework of the law. In
fact, however, subsequent legislation limited such rights
by provisions that were gradually suffocating most of
the missionary schools.

Another consequence of the resurgent nationalism
was hostility toward foreigners, large numbers of whom
were forced to leave the country between 1932 and
1934. It should be observed here that very many of these
emigrants were Christians.

Up to the time of the Kemalist revolution Turkey had
been an Islamic theocracy. Kemal Ataturk and his
friends attributed the country's backwardness to the
determining influence of the religion of Mohammet.
Hence they drew a line of separation between religion
and the State, which became even more marked in 1928,
when Article 2, which declared Islamism to be the State
religion, disappeared from the Constitution. The *Sceria*,
the holy law of the Moslem religion, was abandoned for
modern legislation: the Swiss civil law, the Italian penal

code, and German commercial law were introduced. This secularization destroyed the privileged status enjoyed by the Islamic religion and the Caliphate itself was suppressed in 1924 by a vote of the Great Assembly.

The effects of the new policy were felt not only by the Moslems but by the Christian groups. The religious leaders of the minorities were, in fact, also the civil leaders of the various communities which on the basis of a centuries-old tradition had "personal statutes" which, according to the Treaty of Lausanne, the Turkish government was obliged to respect. But due to the infiltration of its agents into the most important communities of religious minorities, the government was able to obtain the "spontaneous" renunciation of these personal statutes on the part of those leaders who then subjected themselves to the common law. From a legal point of view, therefore, all citizens became equal before the law. But this equality was theoretical because Christians were always regarded with suspicion, excluded from public office as well as certain private employment, forbidden to practice many trades and hampered in business. This was why many Greeks in Constantinople began to emigrate to Athens.[4]

As we have seen the situation of Christianity in Turkey in general and Catholicism in particular was critical. There did, however, exist the legal possibility, more theoretical than real, that Catholics could obtain civil rights equal to those which the state recognized with

[4] Cf. Gugielmo De Vries, S.J.: "Catholicism and the Religious Problem in the Near East" in *La Civiltà Cattolica*, Rome, 1944.

respect to other religious communities. In Turkey, Mons. Roncalli had to show that Catholicism was not hostile to the independence of peoples and to their evolution toward higher forms of civilization and social life, and that, on the contrary, it encouraged every orderly evolution in this sense.

Naturally we cannot know the exact directives of the mission entrusted to Mons. Angelo Giuseppe Roncalli. It is not difficult, however, to reconstruct the principles that inspired it if we bear in mind that the "policy" of Pius XI was constantly geared to bringing Catholicism, with its authentic universal spirit, to all peoples. Particular attention was paid to those who were adopting modern political forms after centuries of more or less indirect dependence on other nations, and who wished for progress in their own ways and traditions.

In this as in many other matters the pontificate of Achille Ratti was a continuation of that of Benedict XV. It is well known, for example, that in Russia when the privileged status of the Orthodox Church came to an end with Czarism and the separation of Church and State was declared, the Vatican for a time entertained the idea that the religious penetration of a world up to then hermetically sealed off to Catholic expansion, was not impossible. The fruit of this generous idea, as is known, was the "Russian College" established in Rome in 1929 with the purpose of preparing priests of the Eastern rite destined for the apostolate on Russian territory. It is also known that Pius XI, following the attempts of his predecessors to establish diplomatic relations with modern China which had been frustrated by the opposition of the French, sent to Peking the first apostolic delegate of the Holy See, the future Cardinal Celso Costantini. The Holy Father also consecrated the first Chinese bishops in 1925.

Archbishop Roncalli had to demonstrate that the Catholic faith is universal and therefore supra-national and unconcerned with earthly matters, and that because of its very universalism it respects and protects the aspirations of various peoples, encouraging what is most noble in them.

The spirit underlying those efforts of Pius XI and his Apostolic Delegate was very aptly expressed by the remarks of a French missionary made at the time: "I will make my schools Turkish; and I will be in less of a hurry to hang the Crucifix, which I venerate, on its walls, than to establish the idea of loyal service, elevation of thought, and aspiration toward the higher things of life so that when the name of Our Lord is pronounced there will be no lack of an echoing response in the souls of the students."

The great powers, especially France, were not enthusiastic over this new policy of the Holy See. An Italian historian, a non-Catholic, and of secularist orientation writes:

"The maintenance of the French protectorate over Catholics in the East was one of the questions dealt with by France and the Holy See before the resumption of diplomatic relations in 1924. The French deplored the fact that the Holy See entered into direct relations with the Turkish government in Constanti-

nople and Ankara, by sending Mons. Marmaggi there
in 1922 and Mons. Filippi in 1923, and regarded this as
a violation of French rights. Other complaints were
made following the accrediting of an apostolic delegate, Mons. Costantini, to Peking. Another act of the
Holy See which was held to be injurious to French interests was the transfer from Lyons to Rome of the
headquarters of the Society for the Propagation of the
Faith. . . . Papal Rome reveals a tendency to make missionary activities more completely ecclesiastical and
supra-national, so as to remove the propagation of the
Catholic faith in non-European countries from a framework reflecting the political disputes of the different
nations." [5]

Apart from a minor inaccuracy (apostolic delegates
do not have a diplomatic status, hence they are not "accredited") Professor Salvatorelli recognizes the reality
of facts. And it is within the frame of this reality that
Mons. Angelo Roncalli's mission in Turkey must be
considered.

The simultaneous mission to Greece entrusted to
Mons. Roncalli was no easier. The Catholics who were
either voluntarily or involuntarily leaving Turkey were
mostly of Greek origin, and they sought refuge in their
country of origin. But here they encountered new religious problems. If, in general, those who belonged to
the Latin rite were received without great difficulty,
Catholics of the Greek rite were exposed to the suspicion of the dissident ecclesiastical authorities (Ortho-

[5] Luigi Salvatorelli: *La Politica della Santa Sede dopo la Guerra, Milan,* pp. 111–13.

dox) who opposed the presence of Catholic priests of the Byzantine rite on Greek territory.

The Catholic exarchate of Constantinople established in 1911, included all Greece by 1923 because the mass emigration of Greeks from Thrace and from those living in Istanbul pointed up the necessity of caring for these emigrants. In 1932 the exarchate was divided: Mons. George Calavassy was entrusted with the pastoral care of the Catholics of the Byzantine rite in all of Greece, and Mons. Dionysius Varouchas with those of the Byzantine rite (therefore not the Melkites and the Armenians) who had remained in the Turkish Republic. Monsignor Calavassy had to struggle strenuously against the claims of the Orthodox ecclesiastical authorities and he won his battle after a series of court trials that gained him a notable popularity, especially in Greek intellectual circles.

From 1934 onward Monsignor Angelo Giuseppe Roncalli concerned himself especially with the problem of the Catholics of the Eastern rite in Greece, in close collaboration with the exarch, Mons. George Calavassy. Their hope was that the Catholics of the Eastern rite in Athens would obtain recognition of their civil rights on a par with other religious groups.

The task, we repeat, was not an easy one. For one reason, as has been said, apostolic delegates have no diplomatic status, hence they are not accredited to governments. Their task is to keep watch over the conditions of the Church in the territory which has been entrusted to them, and to keep the Pope informed.

The only thing that they can do directly is to work

within the Catholic communities in order to see that no
disputes with the civil authorities arise, and that possible
misunderstandings are coped with immediately and before they get out of hand. Thus it is only indirectly,
through personal contact, that they can support, if possible, their strictly religious activity.

It is a fact that during his mission in Turkey Mons.
Roncalli did not have contact with the Turkish government. His relations with the official authorities were
limited to a formal courtesy call on them which Monsignor Roncalli repeated every time he returned to Turkey from a trip to Greece. On such occasions he would
leave his calling card with the President of the Republic,
with the Head of the Government, and with the Minister of Foreign Affairs.

His friendship with Menemengioglu did not begin
either at Ankara or Istanbul, but in Paris much later.
The Turkish Ambassador, who in his native country
had always officially ignored the existence of the Apostolic Delegate, became his greatest admirer and sup-
porter among the diplomatic corps in the French capital. This was not only because Mons. Roncalli's activity
in Turkey, viewed in the perspective of time, merited
the esteem of the Turkish authorities, but also because
this gave the ambassador an opportunity to point out his
country's importance.

"Look," he would say, "when the Vatican wants to
train a great nuncio, where does it send him? To Turkey!"

In Istanbul the Apostolic Delegate had some contact
with the members of the diplomatic corps whom he

now and then invited to the headquarters of the Delegation in small groups of three or four. Women members of the various foreign colonies were never invited to the little villa of Pera, but they were received in the summer residence of the Delegation on Prinkipo island on the Bosporus.

Monsignor Roncalli's activity was then primarily pastoral, an activity he carried out with a spiritual and material charity that was practically limitless. Those who were near him in those years say that he gave away everything he had. When he went out he always dressed like a simple clergyman and was accompanied by his secretary or a domestic servant.

Visits to artistic monuments or to bazaars, where he often stopped in the shops of dealers in antiques, were his only diversions. Mons. Roncalli's bibliophilism goes back a long time and he always found a particular fascination in poring over old books and manuscripts. In the bazaar of Istanbul he would stop to talk with old De Gregori, an Italian somehow stranded in Istanbul who managed to make a living selling old books. Apart from the pleasure of speaking Italian with him, Signor Gregori amused him because he knew nothing whatsoever about the books he was selling.

"Look, Monsignore, what a big beautiful book. It must weigh at least twelve pounds!"

According to the young secretaries who worked with him at different times, living with him was like being at home with their own families. One of them, Father Thomas Ryan, now Monsignor Ryan and a councilor of nunciature, is a tall, powerfully built Irishman, all muscle. In his speeches he was often not too tender toward non-Catholics.

"Oh, you Irish!" Mons. Roncalli would say to him, "as soon as you come into the world, even before you are baptized, you begin to fire away at Protestants!"

Father Thomas was and still is a great smoker, and in the summer he was in the habit of quenching his thirst with beer.

"A day will come," the delegate told him once, "when a doctor will say: 'No more smoking and no more beer if you want to enjoy a long life.' "

Monsignor Ryan, who had just finished his spiritual exercises, replied, "When that terrible moment comes, Excellency, I will say, Jesus have mercy on me!"

Archbishop Roncalli smoked one cigarette after meals, only to keep his guests company. He found no pleasure in smoking and he would often hold the cigarette aloft between his fingers and good-naturedly observe, "I just can't understand how one can become a slave to a little bit of tobacco wrapped up in a piece of paper."

Signor Davide Cugini of Bergamo tells the story that toward the end of July 1935, he and his wife boarded a ship in Venice for a cruise through the Black Sea. A few days later, on August 2, he arrived at Istanbul where he had to deliver a letter addressed to Mons. Roncalli by some of his Bergamesco friends. Upon arriving at the Delegate's residence in Pera he found him away from home, but the servant urged him and his wife to wait since Mons. Roncalli was expected back momentarily. In fact he did arrive several minutes later.

"As soon as he saw us he asked us to please wait for a minute. I was not surprised at seeing him for the first time in civilian clothes, just like his secretary, because at that time the Turkish government had just issued a decree forbidding the ministers of any cult to wear an ecclesiastical habit in public. . . .

"After a few minutes his servant reappeared and led us to a spacious reception room on the floor above. Mons. Roncalli, who had meanwhile changed his clothes, came forward to meet us with his customary affability, wearing his bishop's habit and insignia. I introduced myself and told him that I had the pleasant task of bringing him news about his father's health. As I pronounced those words it seemed that a veil of sadness fell over his face, a sadness which deepened as he read the letter. Then he looked up at us and, deeply moved, said resignedly:

" 'You have been away from Bergamo for a few days so you can't know that today, unhappily, things are quite different. . . . My poor father might have been better last week, but he suffered a relapse after your departure. I was informed of his death by wire and I am most sorrowful at his loss and at not being beside him when he drew his last breath. But we priests are trained to go far away from our families and to sacrifice family affections for other more serious duties.' "

At such a time, however, Mons. Roncalli could not remain so far away from his home. As soon as it was possible for him to do so, he returned to Sotto il Monte for about a week, in order to pray over the grave of his father together with his brothers. The ties of memory that bound them together were many.

A childhood friend of Angelo Roncalli's, Giacomo Perico, a servant with the Capuchins on Piazza Velasquez in Milan, recalls that when Angelo Roncalli first took leave from his father to go to the seminary in Bergamo, Giovanni Battista was turning over the soil with a spade. He looked at the boy, then, after lifting the spade from the furrow he stuck it in the ground, handle first. The metal gleamed brilliantly in the sun.

" 'If I could only see you some day with this spade on your head!' said the father suddenly, picking it up and placing it over his son's head.

"The shining spade looked like a silver mitre!"

The father had died thinking about his son, about the bishop in a distant country to whom he would remain united in the Communion of Saints. Angelo felt the sweetness of his father's spiritual presence, as he was to feel it always, especially when many years later in the Sistine Chapel a Cardinal asked him, *"Quomodo vis vocari?"*—How do you wish to be called?

In 1939 while he was still in Istanbul, Mons. Roncalli received news of the death of his mother. The good and pious Marianna Mazzola had also died without the comfort of her son's presence, but she had died kissing one of his letters. Thoughts of the past came to Angelo Roncalli's mind at such a sad moment. He recalled that in 1921 he had returned to Sotto il Monte to celebrate a Mass in the robes of a domestic prelate of His Holi-

Don Angelo Roncalli
Secretary to Bishop Radini-Tedeschi

Sotto il Monte, Birthplace of Angelo Roncalli

Room in which he was born

Giovanni Battista Roncalli
Father of Angelo Roncalli

Angelo Roncalli (center)
as student in
Roman Seminary (1901)

Bishop Radini-Tedeschi of Bergamo

Chaplain Roncalli with his two brothers during World War 1

Archbishop Roncalli
Apostolic Visitor to Bulgaria (1927)

1. gennaio 1945

Nuncio in Paris arriving to present credentials

Papal Nuncio presenting New Year's greetings to General De Gaulle (194

Nuncio Roncalli and Edouard Herriot,
ex-Premier of France

Arrival in Venice as Cardinal Patriarch, March 1953

The Patriarch of Venice congratulates regatta winner (1957)

ness. That same afternoon the women of the village were gathered in the cemetery to recite the rosary and to exchange gossip, and one of them asked Marianna: "What have they done to your son that he now dresses like a bishop?"

"How should I know," replied his mother with her characteristic simplicity, "those are things that priests arrange between themselves."

In Turkey as in Greece, Mons. Roncalli was assisted only by one secretary. For a while a young Lombard priest, Don Angelo Dell' Acqua, worked with him. (This priest is now the Substitute Secretary of State of His Holiness.) Mons. Roncalli had no transportation of his own and in order to get around he used taxis and the public conveyances. This gave him many opportunities to know the Turkish people in the context of their daily lives.

All those who knew him during his Turkish mission have declared that his activity earned him not only the love of the Catholic communities, undergoing a time of bitter trial, but the universal esteem of the Turkish people. Everyone felt the Christian love and human sympathy that were the hallmarks of his character. The cordiality of his manners, the understanding he showed for the views of a nation that was struggling toward rebirth—though not always respecting the equity of others—did not leave unmoved even the hardened Turkish nationalists. In the person of the apostolic delegate they came to a clearer understanding of the universal significance of the Roman pontificate and the value of its mission.

The kind heart and intelligence of Mons. Roncalli were even better revealed during World War II when great efforts were being made by the belligerents on both sides to draw Turkey, one of the crucial areas of the Eastern Mediterranean, into the conflict. The opposing diplomatic staffs worked hard, with all the means at their disposal, to draw neutral Turkey into this or that camp. The Ankara government, for its part, was quite determined to guard and preserve its neutrality. Ankara and Istanbul, therefore, were not only excellent "listening-posts" but scenes of the most subtle diplomatic intrigues. Germany, as is known, was represented by Von Papen who was also the dean of the diplomatic corps.

Mons. Roncalli observed all that went on about him and kept the Holy See informed. But in his advance post he was, above all at that time, the intelligent and indefatigable worker in the relief activities of Pius XII, aimed at limiting or lessening the sufferings of the war.

Immediately following the election of John XXIII, Dr. Isaac Halévy Herzog, the Grand Rabbi of Israel, sent him a congratulatory greeting, in which among other things he said:

"I am persuaded that your noble faith in the highest human values, as shown during the time of the Nazi atrocities, will guide you in your new and important tasks . . ."

The explanation of this is that during that time Mons. Roncalli was in Istanbul, and in that city one could act, if not to prevent the sacrifice of innocent victims of war and persecution, at least to limit this sacrifice and save everyone it was possible to save. The allusion of the Grand Rabbi of Israel was a reminder that the Apostolic Delegate had performed a yeoman service in this sense and that to him thousands of Jews owed their opportunity to escape persecution and to find refuge in Palestine during the most terrible years of the war.

In justice it must be said that in this work the Delegate had the help of Ambassador Von Papen. For this reason toward the end of the war Von Papen was to request the Apostolic Delegate to petition the Holy See to take steps to see that the stern judgment of nations and mankind that was about to fall on Germany for its crimes should distinguish properly between the responsibilities of Nazism and the cause of the German people.

But earlier, in 1941, when Von Papen had asked Mons. Roncalli whether Hitler's war against communism would not produce "a more positive attitude" on the part of the Vatican toward Nazi Germany, the Archbishop had replied calmly but sternly:

"And what answer do you give me regarding the two million and a half Polish Jews that you are exterminating?"

And Greece? The significance of Mons. Angelo Roncalli's mission to Greece has already been explained. And when the disaster of war fell upon the small and proud Mediterranean nation, aid from the Delegate was implored.

On the occasion of his election as Pope, the newspapers in Athens recalled his charitable activities. Later the newspaper *Vima* gave further details regarding

Mons. Roncalli's work in a series of articles. The author, Elias Venezis, stated that he found the documents relative to the Apostolic Delegate's activity while he was looking for material for a biography of the Metropolitan Damaskinos, head of the autocephalic dissident Church. In the spring of 1941, after the occupation, Greece was seriously threatened by famine. It was then that Mons. Roncalli, in the name of the Greek people, proposed to ask the Holy See to urge the Allies to let food be brought into the country. The proposal was gratefully accepted by Bishop Damaskinos and the two prelates met on neutral territory, that is, in the house of a common acquaintance, in order to work out the details of the proposal.

The Apostolic Delegate went to Rome himself to report on the tragic situation of the Greeks. Thereupon the Holy See entered into negotiations with the Allies, especially with England, and obtained permission for ships loaded with provisions to get through the blockade. In this way 360,000 tons of wheat arrived in Greece and were distributed by the Red Cross. At the same time dispensaries of the Pontifical Work of Assistance were opened and were called "Centers of Divine Providence." In addition the Apostolic Delegate intervened frequently with the occupation authorities and saved many lives and avoided or repaired many injustices.

The gratitude of the Greek people for his efforts on their behalf has never been forgotten. It came spontaneously to the fore when the former delegate was elected to the throne of St. Peter. But even before his election, every time that Cardinal Roncalli met Greek Orthodox prelates, they never failed to remind him of the undying appreciation of the Greek people.

An Italian ambassador, Count Dino Secco-Suardi, also a Bergamesco, reports that in Bayreuth, in 1955, he saw the Greek Patriarch come to Cardinal Roncalli, who had arrived as pontifical legate to the Eucharistic Congress, to offer bread in the form used in the oriental rites for his use as a Host in saying his Mass.

The Apostolic Delegate served the spiritual needs not only of the Greek people but of combatants on its soil. An Italian army chaplain, attached to the 64th Infantry Regiment of the Cagliari Division, recalled that in October 1942 the Apostolic Delegate visited the Italian troops at Kalamata in Greece in order to confirm one hundred and ten soldiers. He was awaited with great emotion and greeted with the honors due a division commander.

"But when he got out of the car the soldiers realized that there was nothing military about Mons. Roncalli. Instead, his countenance expressed a compassionate tenderness as if to ask the soldiers' pardon for having disturbed them. The soldiers immediately saw in him a loving Father. . . ."

It was the mission in Bulgaria, Greece and Turkey that formed the diplomat Roncalli. But what is a diplomat? Let us leave the answer to the above-mentioned Ambassador Secco-Suardi who wrote at the time of Pope John's election:

"What is required of a good diplomat? That he believe in the cause he supports, that he understand the cause of others, and that he know how to grasp every possible convergence of interests. And that, finally, through his contacts, treated with tolerance, sympathy and cordiality, he can patiently prepare for and await the day of agreement and understanding. This manner of behavior resembles very much the requirements of Christian charity. Herein lies the deep source of the prestige surrounding the diplomacy of the Church. She has no more of a talisman assuring success than any other institution. But when she loses, she never loses entirely, because she has spent herself with love. This is an old but eternal truth: the great diplomats of the Holy Roman Church are those who are priests above all, and who never for a moment forget their high and unchangeable priestly mission as they walk upon the unsteady terrain of a diplomatic mission.

"In view of a reality so different from the absurd legends of a mysterious, omniscient Vatican diplomacy, mistress of intrigue, the diplomatic figure of Cardinal Roncalli can be understood only by going back to the time of his training in the sacred ministry and to the first proofs of his industry . . . Today everyone admires the enlightenment of his career, but not everyone recalls that he did not arrive at the pinnacles of diplomacy through the usual routine of the State Secretariat and nunciatures but through his virtues, native to him but perfected in the exercise of his pastoral duties in his native country.

"The priestly vocation and the practice of charity are the forces that have guided the seminarian Angelo Roncalli from his humble rural birthplace to the greatest responsibilities of the Church."

V

•••••••••••••••

Papal Nuncio in Paris

IMMEDIATELY FOLLOWING the election of John XXIII, French newspapers, as was natural, expressed their great satisfaction with the event. They recalled the long sojourn of Archbishop Roncalli as papal nuncio in Paris and the sympathy and cordiality he had engendered about him, both in his routine diplomatic contacts with the Quai d'Orsay and with the French political world in general.

One newspaper—there is no need to give its name—reminded its readers of Mons. Roncalli's first encounter with a French government official upon his arrival in Paris on the morning of December 31, 1944. "I am a traveler of God," Mons. Roncalli is said to have announced to the highest functionary at the Elysée Palace who received him that morning in an office which looked more like a dusty den for archives than a reception room in the palace of the President of the French Republic. A vase with a few flowers had been placed on the functionary's table; this was all the sad and divided French

Republic of that time could offer the personage whom Pius XII had nominated apostolic nuncio to Paris.

Mons. Roncalli countered the functionary's distress over this rather sad and unbecoming reception of the Pope's representative with a humorous simplicity so contagious that the functionary began to laugh with him and to forget his embarrassment.

"I love flowers and everything beautiful and gay which God has wished to create in the world," the Nuncio is said to have remarked to the official who received him in the name of the French Republic. "Therefore, if you will permit me I will take along these carnations which I think have been placed on this table for me. And you, dear Sir, please relax and don't worry about a thing. You know I became a nuncio quite by accident."

Then he told the amazed functionary that when he had received the coded message informing him that he had been nominated nuncio to Paris, he had at first thrown the telegram into a drawer of his desk because he had been unable to decipher it and the decoding clerk had been absent. The clerk, Mons. Ryan, had returned two days later, and by then Angelo Roncalli had forgotten about the telegram. And it would have remained even for a longer time in his desk drawer had it not been followed by a telephone call from Vatican City asking him for a reply. Archbishop Roncalli agreed to accept the nomination but with great reluctance.

After having thus relieved the functionary of his distress, he took the flowers and walked toward the exit. The functionary offered to accompany him but Mons.

Roncalli said, "Please don't bother. The ushers will show me to the street. I shall see you again when General De Gaulle gets here."

Newspaper stories of this kind were accompanied by others relating the role that Mons. Roncalli was supposed to have played in preventing the destruction of Paris by the retreating Germans. (Actually they had left the city some four months before his arrival.) All these stories have a certain charm, but they do not correspond with the facts. Many stories and anecdotes about Mons. Roncalli and John XXIII are already in circulation, and often these are complete fabrications. Sometimes, however, there is some merit even to fabrications, at least in this case, because in general this story is very well fitted to the personality of the new Pope.

In reality Archbishop Roncalli had been nominated as apostolic nuncio to France on December 23, 1944. He had received notice of the nomination in a coded message wired to Istanbul, together with orders to proceed by the fastest means possible to his new post, via Rome. It is true that Monsignor Ryan had been temporarily absent. But Mons. Roncalli had an inkling of the purport of the message, although in truth the idea of sending him to Paris appeared far-fetched and unreal. When the message was fully decoded, Mons. Roncalli's first impression was confirmed. He left Istanbul immediately, and upon arriving in Rome he met Mons. Tardini by chance in the Cortile de San Damaso. The first thing he said to him was to ask "if perchance they have all gone crazy?"

"Dear Monsignore," replied Mons. Tardini, "you

may be sure that the idea didn't come from any one of us. Go to the Pope."

Archbishop Roncalli asked for an audience and presented himself to Pius XII. As soon as he saw him the Pope said: "We want you to know that the idea of nominating you was Ours." And indeed so it was.

It came about in this manner. The apostolic nuncio, now Cardinal Valerio Valeri, had been in France during the war, and after the tragic events of 1940 had followed the fleeing government to Vichy. Nuncio Valeri could not have done otherwise than to follow the government to which he was accredited and which was considered by most to be the legitimate one. There had been nothing in Archbishop Valeri's attitude that could be considered other than respectful to the French nation, and besides it was not his place to express judgment or to assume an attitude of agreement or disagreement.

On coming to power, the new Provisional Government, headed by General De Gaulle, asked for the recall of Mons. Valeri. Because he had been at Vichy, De Gaulle could only request his recall, a request which he nevertheless mingled with praise and sincere regrets. The new government, however, was insistent in its demands for a new nuncio, and that he be assigned before January 1, 1945.

It is a French tradition that the head of the State receive the New Year greetings of the diplomatic corps and these are presented by the dean on behalf of his colleagues. Since the Congress of Vienna (1815) it has been a convention accepted by many countries that the apostolic nuncio, regardless of seniority, is always the dean of the diplomatic corps.

The French reasoning in this case was that in the absence of a papal nuncio, the dean of the diplomatic corps would be the Soviet ambassador, whose duty it would then be to express the New Year wishes in the name of all the ambassadors. Such a situation would be distasteful to the French people. Hence repeated requests for a new nuncio were made personally to Pope Pius XII, who then nominated Archbishop Roncalli.

The latter remained in Rome only for the time necessary to prepare his credentials and to receive instructions regarding the new and difficult mission that awaited him. Then he hastened to Paris in a French military aircraft, arriving on December 31, 1944. On the very next morning he was at the Elysée Palace to present his credentials and to formulate, as dean of the diplomatic corps, the New Year greetings to the President of the Provisional Government, General Charles De Gaulle.

The importance of Mons. Roncalli's arrival in Paris in time for the New Year ceremony explains his extremely rapid journey from the Bosporus to the Seine and the brevity of his stay in Rome. Naturally, he could not go to Bergamo to see his family, from whom he had been away for so long, since Northern Italy was still occupied by the Germans.

When Mons. Angelo Giuseppe Roncalli presented his letters of credentials as apostolic nuncio in Paris to the President of the Provisional French Government on January 1, 1945, memories of his youth came forth even in

his address of greeting to General De Gaulle, and the
memory of Mons. Radini entered the halls of the Elysée
Palace along with him:

"In presenting Your Excellency with the letters which
accredit me as Nuncio to the President of the Provisional
Government of the French Republic, my thoughts go
back spontaneously to the distant days of my young
priesthood during which, at the school of a great bishop
who contributed so much in Italy to an appreciation of
the spiritual grandeurs of France, I learned to know and
love your country. Called later to the Higher Council of
the Society for the Propagation of the Faith, and then to
represent the Supreme Pontiff in Bulgaria and Turkey,
my sincere affection and my profound admiration could
but grow as daily I saw before my eyes the magnificent
spectacle of this France whose spirit knows no frontiers
and whose generous activities have been carried across
the entire world by the dedication of her sons, in particular by her missionaries.

"Your Excellency can therefore appreciate the feelings with which I begin the mission that the Holy Father
has deigned to entrust to me in a nation over which there
has swept a war leaving devastation and ruin in its wake
but which, as is demonstrated by the vitality of her re-
surgence, could not darken the splendor of its genius nor
arrest the drive of her soul, by which the most generous
acts are considered as simple and ordinary.

"But even more than expressing these feelings I am
obliged on this occasion to present to Your Excellency
the pledge of esteem and affection with which the Holy
Father has charged me, together with the assurance of
his particular benevolence for your country.

"To this pledge of my august Sovereign permit me, Your Excellency, to add those which I make to you in the living hope that I, with the help of God and the precious cooperation of your Government, will be allowed to draw even closer the existing relations between the Holy See and the noble French nation."

Following the presentation of credentials, Mons. Roncalli, in the name of the diplomatic corps, extended New Year greetings to the President of the Provisional Government in part as follows:

". . . In the midst of inevitable ordeals and sufferings the year that is now coming to a close is marked in France by events of the greatest importance. Thanks to your far-seeing statesmanship and your energy, this beloved country has again found its freedom and its faith in its own destinies. We do not doubt that the coming year will witness new progress and new events. Thus France regains her traditional physiognomy and her rightful place among nations. With her lucid spirit, her love of work, her love of freedom, and with her spiritual splendor of which I saw so many evidences during many years spent in the Near East, she will know how to point out the way to a unity of hearts and a spirit of justice that may lead our society toward an era of tranquility and peace. This is the exhortation which in these days comes from on high. May it be listened to by all men of good will. . . ."

The tasks awaiting the apostolic nuncio were not simple. France, reunited by the liberation, was deeply divided in spirit. This had happened, to a different degree, in all European countries involved in a war which, in ad-

dition to sorrow and ruin, had brought with it political
upheavals and serious crises of conscience.

France has a very old tradition of unity and along with
it a patriotic feeling solidly rooted in the common spirit
of the people. But the moral breaches of the war years
had wounded the national pride, embittered by foreign
occupation and by indignation directed against those
who had seemed to collaborate with the German invaders. Today an outsider, and one who looks at the French
situation of that period in the perspective of time, could
assert that even the French who approved of Pétain and
supported the Vichy regime loved their country and
had acted as they had because they believed that this was
the only way to salvage what was salvageable of the material and moral interests of France.

The fundamental error lay in the initial political eval-
uation of the situation. Marshall Pétain was a great soldier, and a brave and competent general. But generals,
especially in old Europe, do not always possess political
talents. Napoleon Bonaparte, a very great soldier but perhaps even a greater politician, was an exception.

In the days after the fall of France a man with a very
fine sense of political intuition and about whom the
world was to hear a great deal later, Alcide de Gasperi,
said that France's basic error was to have given herself
a military leader.

"Military men," declared De Gasperi, who then was
employed in the Vatican Library, "believe that there is
nothing more to do once they have been defeated on the
battlefield. France still has many valuable cards to play:
Corsica and North Africa. But Pétain will not play them.

Having been beaten militarily he considers himself defeated and will conduct himself like a vanquished foe."

In 1940 Pétain believed that a Nazi victory was imminent and inevitable and that the path he had taken was the only one possible. His collaborators shared this view as did not a few Frenchmen. It was not accidental, for example, that ultranationalists like Charles Maurras were with him. They too felt that there was no other way to save something of eternal France from the wreckage.

Supporting Pétain were also certain conservative Catholics belonging to the middle and upper bourgeoisie who had given many good Christian soldiers to their country. In certain cases such persons were still sympathetic to Maurras' *Action Française* despite the papal condemnation of the organization and the bitter campaign that the monarchist newspaper of the same name had conducted in the pre-war years against Pius XI, whom it had called "the most German pope in history," and against the apostolic nuncio, Archbishop Maglione, "the Vatican spy." One of the great ironies of history was that those once proud foes of Germany and Germanism were now collaborating with German Nazis.

Public opinion turned against Pétain and the Vichy government as military operations gradually made it clear that the *blitzkrieg* was an illusion of Hitler and his marshals. When people began to understand that a German victory was no longer as certain as it had seemed, the first signs of restiveness and protest were registered; at first by passive attitudes, later by active resistance. This took place after the aerial battle over London and the failure of the Germans to land in England, and especially after the attack on Russia and the intervention of the United States. Another contributing factor, of course, was that the yoke of the occupation was becoming increasingly heavier to bear. The prestige of Free France, of General De Gaulle, and of his companions who had kept the faith when most others had despaired grew with each development. Thus was born the Resistance and the *maquis*.

General Pétain and the men of Vichy, partly because of their characters, their moral and religious education, partly perhaps because of political calculation, had rejected the anticlerical secularism that had been the mark of the Third French Republic. They had granted the Church some freedoms which heretofore had been denied her, in other words, a *rapprochement* had taken place between the Vichy regime and the Catholic Church and the ecclesiastical hierarchy.

Given this *rapprochement* one may ask: were the bishops favorable to Pétain? This was asserted at the end of the war when it became necessary to fix the blame, real or alleged, for the recent past.

In reality during those difficult years the bishops had remained at their posts with all the moral steadfastness called for by the circumstances. The Church requires her pastors never to abandon their flocks, above all in situations of crisis; consequently the bishops, in view of their very mission, could not avoid contacts with the civil powers, whether or not these were legitimate or merely *de facto*.

When, in September 1945, the tribunal of Zagreb sentenced Archbishop Stepinac, now a Cardinal, the indom-

itable Yugoslav Archbishop had made the following declaration before his judges:

"You accuse me of being an enemy of the state and the
people's power. Will you tell me who my civil authorities were in 1941? Perhaps Simovich in Belgrade or the
government in exile in London which you call traitor-
ous, or that in Palestine, or you yourselves at that time
living in the midst of the forests. For me you became
the state power as of May 8, 1945. Could I, perhaps,
have obeyed you when you were hiding in the forests,
and at the same time obey those in Zagreb? You cannot
serve two masters. This conforms neither with the principles of morality nor with international law nor with
simple human rights. We could not but take into account
the established power in Zagreb, even though this power
was Ustachi.[1] This was the ruling power. . . ."

This speech may also serve as a defense of the French
bishops during the dramatic war years, although conditions in France were not as tragic as those in Yugoslavia.
But was there any sympathy among them for the old
Marshal who, despite his years, had agreed to serve his
nation? The answer to this question is that it is not impossible that some elements of the clergy did nourish
sentiments of this character. Nonetheless, the French
bishops always and in every case did their duty, nor were
they silent when the laws of God or the rights of people
were disregarded or trampled upon.

At the end of the war when France, under De Gaulle,
arose from its sorrows and left the ranks of the van-

[1] Fiorelli Cavalli: *The Case against the Archbishop of Zagreb*, Rome,
1947, p. 151.

quished to enter those of the victors, some Catholics in France were asked to account for their attitude during the occupation or under the Vichy regime. Tremendous pressure was exerted in order to have certain bishops "spontaneously" renounce their dioceses, for them to retire to private life and relinquish their posts to others.

In this new situation the old polemics again came to the fore. Catholic democrats, the Catholics of the so-called Left, who had fought in the underground war for national liberation, were very severe toward their co-religionists who were considered to be conservative or even nationalist, and some of whom had not hesitated to compromise themselves with the Vichy regime and with the German invaders. Now they were called on to settle both the old scores and the new. Such attitudes were not alien to the controversy over the bishops. To judge the state of mind prevalent in those years it is enough to re-call that an effort was made to drive from his see the then Archbishop of Bordeaux who is none other than the present Maurice Cardinal Feltin, Archbishop of Paris, loved and esteemed not only by his colleagues in the French episcopate and by the faithful, but by all persons capable of appreciating his intelligence, charity and goodness.

There was in France a prelate whom the men of the Resistance favored because of his attitude toward German racism. He was Mons. Jules Saliège, Archbishop of Toulouse. He had been paralyzed for many years and talked only with great difficulty, but he did not keep silent in the face of the racist persecutions imposed by the Nazis. In the days immediately following the election of John XXIII, an Italian political leader, Giuseppe Saragat, who had represented defeated Italy in Paris in the immediate post-war period, related that it was he who had indicated to Nuncio Roncalli the Provisional French Government's desire to see the fearless archbishop elevated to the cardinalate. Saragat, now secretary of the Italian Social-Democratic party, said that Mons. Roncalli did not wait for the hint to be repeated.

It is a fact that at the papal consistory of February 1946, Mons. Saliège was created a cardinal of the Holy Roman Church, and the Nuncio himself presented him with the cardinal's red biretta. This does not mean to say that Mons. Roncalli had to await the hint of the Italian representative before recommending Mons. Saliège's elevation. Saragat's testimony is interesting because it is a recognition of the Nuncio's sagacity and to his readiness to rise to the occasion whenever this was possible without harm to justice or charity.

Upon his arrival in Paris the Nuncio had to face the problem of the controversies concerning certain bishops —one of great seriousness and delicacy—without opposing the French government and, at the same time, without offending the hierarchy. He knew how to keep the question outside the heated polemical atmosphere of the immediate post-war period, and how to infuse a spirit of calm into the members of the government and a spirit of submission among the bishops. Some of the latter (three in all) renounced their dioceses, but not as many as was desired by the civil authorities, in particular the Minister of Foreign Affairs who at that time was the Catholic Georges Bidault.

Apostolic nuncios, in addition to representing the Pope, also have the task of assuring direct contacts between the national hierarchies and the Holy See. Thus Mons. Roncalli could exercise his mission—evangelical in this case and not political—among the bishops. His task was one of mediation and peace-making. The knot of difficulties was untied without any bitterness and without resentments.

The French bishops, many of whom were outstanding for their abilities and noble pastoral life, felt that the Pope's envoy was a sure friend, a colleague even more than the representative of the supreme authority. It is a fact that the French episcopate was and still is very fond of Angelo Roncalli. It is known that at the conclave which elevated him to the supreme pontificate, the French cardinals were the first to launch and support his candidacy.

A press photographer, who was taking pictures of the cardinals as they were leaving the Vatican at the end of one of their general assemblies before the conclave, swears that he heard Cardinal Feltin say to him, "Don't miss Roncalli, he's our Pope." Questioned about this after the election, the Archbishop of Paris replied that he did not remember this incident. But it is certain that the French cardinals were the first supporters of Roncalli's candidacy, especially after Cardinal Valeri was insistent in urging that his own name not be considered.

It is significant that Angelo Giuseppe Roncalli's predecessor in the nunciature to France, who had to leave after the collapse of 1944, left an unforgettable memory of himself in France, linked to feelings of profound esteem and affection. Cerretti, Maglione, Valeri, Roncalli—four nuncios of the first magnitude and later cardinals—worthily continued the great traditions of papal diplomacy on French soil.

If the times were politically difficult, they were no less so from a religious aspect. During the Lenten season of 1947 there appeared a pastoral letter written by the Archbishop of Paris, Cardinal Suhard, which set forth succinctly the most acute problems faced by Catholicism. The document, entitled "Growth or Decline of the Church?" pointed out that World War II had marked the end of one world, and the beginning of another. At the war's termination, due to the discoveries of science and the growth of means of communication, humanity had entered a new era which was to elaborate a universalistic civilization. Who would give unity to this humanity? Could the Church ignore a new human reality the outlines of which were already so clear? Some Catholics were saying that truth always triumphs in the end and that in the meantime the best and most fitting thing for the Church to do was to shun all innovations. Other Catholics maintained the contrary: the Church must make modifications in her methods of evangelization in order to participate in shaping the future; she could not remain aloof from the times, as her own history teaches us.

The Cardinal Archbishop suggested a "middle way" between static integralism on one hand and a too adventurous modernism on the other. While laying down a firm and inflexible line in matters of doctrinal truth he urged that the action of Christians, while supernatural before all else, should be adapted to the times. "Adaptation," wrote Cardinal Suhard, "does not mean accommodation, or systematically substituting the 'new' for the 'old,' still less mutilation of the Church's message, but solely an integral and intelligent 'Incarnation' of that message in the actual state of things we have to change." Such an apostolate of "Incarnation" was to be the basis of Catholic action and to be directed above all toward the working class now cut off from the Church. Hence a new form of missionary apostolate was indicated.

The problems to which the Archbishop of Paris referred during the 1947 Lenten season had long been apparent in France. The year 1942 had seen the rise of the first "home mission" movements directed toward the masses which could no longer be reached through the traditional means established by the Church. Large numbers of the people, especially among the workers, had abandoned religion and it was useless to wait for them to return to the churches, called there by a voice they could no longer hear. It had become necessary to go to them, understand their feelings, correct them, and to act in such a way that by degrees their minds once again be opened to the truth. Naturally these new missionary movements, already in existence and to which Cardinal Suhard gave substantial encouragement, were conceived within the framework of realities in France: they would not have taken the same form elsewhere under other religious conditions.

Cardinal Suhard's ideas, which were a summary of those of his predecessor, Cardinal Verdier, had since

1942 found expression in the "Mission de France." This was the "worker-priests" movement which eventually aroused the Holy See's concern and apprehension, and which for that matter also engendered many misgivings in the mind of Cardinal Suhard himself shortly before his death.

With Mons. Angelo Roncalli, as we have seen, the missionary vocation was always latent. In Bulgaria, Turkey, and Greece he had witnessed with profound sorrow the loss of religion and the divorce between a great part of the people and the spiritual treasures which the separated churches of the East still preserve as a precious patrimony. He had long been convinced that the Church must do everything to heal the breach that was developing between truth and life, and that the Church should go to the people and let herself be heard by them. This was one of the teachings imparted to him many years before by Mons. Radini-Tedeschi, and by Professor Giuseppe Toniolo who had already perceived the urgency of this need at the beginning of the century.

Mons. Roncalli, therefore, could understand and share the pastoral preoccupations of the French episcopate. An acute observer of human conditions, he well realized that in France, on the periphery of a Catholicism that was alive both intellectually and spiritually, there were large masses of non-believers and people indifferent to religion. Even before the advent of communism these masses of non-believers had been formed by the anti-religious teachings of the Voltairian philosophers who for at least two generations had undermined the religious conscience of Frenchmen. Anti-clericalism was no longer as acute or strident as it once was. But the shrill, militant hatred (which is at least a negative form of recognition) had in large circles been replaced by an attitude of indifference to religion, no longer hated because it was not even known. This is de-Christianization.

The zeal of these missionaries who carried the faith to pagans without leaving their country undoubtedly came from generous impulses. But the movement gave rise to many serious incidents which finally called for the intervention of the Holy See. It will be recalled that the worker-priests, i.e., priests who became workers in order to redeem workers, exercised an undeniable influence among the laboring classes. But this zeal also led to distortions which in some cases did not render the worker-priests immune to the so-called *mystique* of Marxism and to the practical action which logically derives from it.

Naturally the Apostolic Nuncio could not approve such phenomena nor, for that matter, could they be approved by the French episcopate. But knowledgeable as he was about the French situation, Mons. Roncalli, for as long as he remained in Paris, hoped that the French bishops would restore order to the more dangerous and, in some cases, frankly condemnable attitudes, by a policy of moderation that would injure nobody's sensibilities. In view of the sensitivity of the French, he feared that too direct an interference might provoke bitter and resentful reactions, as it actually did later. Perhaps it was his hope that the experiment would gradually come to an end by itself or by a decision of the French bishops.

After the election of Cardinal Angelo Roncalli to the

chair of St. Peter, many newspaper accounts reported
that he had approved the experiment of the worker-
priests when he was Nuncio in Paris. But when Cardinal Feltin was interviewed in regard to this question,
he was much less explicit and made it clear that the
Nuncio had not given his absolute approval:

". . . I am convinced that a missionary apostolate in
the workers' world is as necessary as one in distant
lands; even the workers' world is far away from us.
Pius XII judged that our movement of worker-priests
was not the one best adapted to achieve this aim and
he requested us to reflect further in order to find other
means. His Holiness is aware of this problem which pre-
occupies us and he knows the difficulties surrounding
it. He was made aware of all this when he was Nuncio
in Paris by my predecessor, Cardinal Suhard. However,
he has never expressed any opinion. Soon we shall ask
John XXIII about what can be done; we shall tell him
of our experiences and we will tell him what our intentions are. And if he does not approve, we shall think
about the matter further and seek for the right form of
approach to this problem. . . ." [2]

As Nuncio, Angelo Giuseppe Roncalli was not one
of those diplomats who wait to be informed or briefed
by intermediaries. He was always convinced that the
most direct and persuasive information is that which one
gathers directly by observing men and affairs in person.
Thus it was always his first concern to learn the language of the country to which he had been sent on a

[2] Interview with Cardinal Feltin in *Epoca*, an illustrated magazine published in Milan, November 9, 1958.

mission. In fact, apart from French, which most Italians know, well or badly, he speaks Bulgarian, Turkish, modern Greek and even Russian.

Knowledge of the language is an indispensable key for discovering the real situation in a country and among its people; the other means to achieve this is to know places and people well. Wherever he happened to be on a mission Mons. Roncalli traveled widely and, if what is said be true, his love of travel did not always arouse the enthusiasm of his ecclesiastical superiors in Rome. He went to Algeria and traveled as far as Constantina. He visited as many places as he could in France, accepting all invitations and talking with everybody. Some French wits, critical and cynical, asked whether Archbishop Roncalli was the apostolic nuncio or a French curé. But Don Angelo let them talk and did not allow himself to be distressed by news that his itinerant diplomacy disturbed certain people rooted in old ways and customs that to him seemed anachronistic.

The fact is, however, that he knows France and the countries in which he was on mission very well, as well as others which he visited during holidays. And as we know, between 1921 and 1924 when he was engaged in missionary work, he traveled throughout Italy and other countries of Europe. In fact, after his election many pilgrims were amazed to hear him speak of their respective homelands with such sure knowledge.

Angelo Roncalli—as has already been said—has the gift of arousing feelings of sympathy and friendship at first sight, and of immediately winning the trust of his interlocutors. In addition, he can be a fascinating con-

versationalist and talk most intelligently and perceptively on the most varied topics and problems without
at the same time letting escape from his lips any imprudent confidences. He says only what he intends to
say. This is not a pose with him; he has always managed
to reconcile the reserve of the diplomat with the cordiality of his ways, and a warm, open and simple manner
of speech. It was this constant amiability to everyone,
his extraordinary priestly character, his courteous behavior that opened all doors to him and won a profound
sympathy for him in France as elsewhere.

His is a deep and up-to-date culture, even though his
historical and humanist interests lead him to seek the
less explored aspects of ancient and modern literatures.
In some of his New Year addresses, as dean of the diplomatic corps, he liked to quote from the French classics.
In his address of 1952, for example, he put together a
delightful anthology of passages from French writers
referring to Christmas. "I have gathered, Mr. President,
some flowers—flowers of Bethlehem—in your garden,"
he said on this occasion. And in the following year he
began the traditional New Year address with a quotation
from La Fontaine.

It was not an unusual sight in Paris between 1945 and
1953 to see an elderly priest conversing amiably but
authoritatively with the *bouquinistes* who sell rare books
and prints along the banks of the Seine. This was none
other than the apostolic nuncio, Mons. Roncalli, on the
verge of an unexpected find. He would also make long
stops in the shops of Paris dealers in antique and rare objects. It was in one of these that he discovered a most

valuable hymnal of the fifteenth century, a parchment
manuscript made up of 152 folios in Gothic script, containing 30 designs in miniature and 166 exquisitely decorated initial letters. Mons. Roncalli immediately realized
that the precious codex had been copied, decorated
and illustrated for the use of the monastery of St. Grata
"in Columnellis," in Bergamo and in some mysterious
way had ended up in France. The hymnal was on sale,
and with the help of two fellow-Bergamascos living in
Paris he bought it and presented it as a gift to the Bishop
of Bergamo, Mons. Bernareggi, to enrich the art collection of the city and the diocese.

The son of peasants knew very well how to represent
the traditional humanism of the Roman Curia in the salon
of the Elysée Palace as well as to take part in intellectual
conversations in Paris drawing rooms. It is therefore
quite understandable that many French intellectuals
have declared their pride and pleasure in having been
his friends. Even the rather hard-to-please François Mauriac was seized with a spirit of elation at the news of his
election:

". . . This is my good fortune! I knew only one
Italian in the Sacred College and he is the very one who
has been chosen. It's true that I share this honor with
many Parisians. One could not be more affable than
he is. Cardinal Roncalli comes from the people and he
has preserved much of the simplicity and goodness of
the people—would not dare to say their gentleness.
This Holy Father will truly be a Father. And so far as
finesse is concerned, I swear to you this he has." [3]

[3] *Express,* Paris, October 30, 1958.

Another French Academician, Count Wladimir d'Ormesson, for some years ambassador to the Vatican, expressed his pleasure in these words: "Cardinal Roncalli whom we have known is essentially a good, a fine and frank man, possessing a profound and gentle knowledge of humanity." [4]

All those who presented themselves at the nunciature, no matter who they were, were certain of receiving a paternal and generous welcome. So generous, in fact, that at a certain point it became necessary to protect Mons. Roncalli from visitors who came in search of material assistance: he would have given away everything he had without the slightest hesitation. This was the reason that Mons. Boleslao Skiladz, the second secretary of the nunciature, was assigned the task of screening these visitors.

The Polish monsignor, who died in November 1958 following an automobile accident, acquitted himself of this task with tact and Christian charity. On November 29, 1958, when John XXIII received Cardinal Wyszynski and the members of the Polish colony in Rome he referred to his faithful secretary with fatherly affection: "In your presence we would like to recall a dear priest who assisted us with generosity and intelligence during several years of our mission in France. Now he is no longer among the living, having died tragically while engaged in an errand of charity. We invoke God's mercy on him and the reward of the just. . . ."

One day two ecclesiastics presented themselves at the little building on Avenue President Wilson. They

[4] Figaro, October 30, 1958.

had come from Rome and were bound for the nunciature in Dublin, but on arriving in Paris they found there was no place for them on the plane leaving for London. Naturally they went to Mons. Roncalli's residence and met him just as he was about to go out. They explained their situation to the Nuncio who, waving his arms toward the house, said warmly, "But this is the house of the Father. Come in, come in! We shall see each other tonight." And that night he sat up until a very late hour with the two pilgrims discussing with them the latest news which they had brought from Rome.

On another occasion Mons. Josef Zabkar, a member of the diplomatic service of the Holy See, fell ill during his stay in Paris. He was a guest at the nunciature for fifteen days during which time Archbishop Roncalli visited him twice daily, bringing him little gifts and affably engaging him in conversation.

In addition to his disarming simplicity, the Nuncio's wit was very acute and he was usually ready with a telling rejoinder. Once taking the floor at a cultural meeting attended by many Jews, he touched upon Biblical questions, making frequent references to Abraham, Isaac and other patriarchs. As the meeting was breaking up, several of those present surrounded him and one of their number complimented him on the perfect knowledge of the Old Testament of which he had just given evidence.

"Ah yes," replied Mons. Roncalli, "I also know the Old Testament, but whenever it is a question of testaments it's the last one that really counts."

Often there were people who thought they were being shrewd when they were only being importunate.

During an election year a politician asked the Nuncio if it were true that the Vatican was supporting the Popular Republican Movement—the French version of the Christian Democratic Party—and opposing the De Gaullist group. Without losing his composure in the slightest, Mons. Roncalli replied:

"Dear sir, just as at the end of the Lenten season all the holy images in the churches are covered with a violet veil, please permit a Nuncio to cover himself with a veil during an election campaign."

He knew some of the weaknesses of the French character (what people doesn't have them?) which is inclined to divide foreigners into two categories: those who love France and those who do not.

The Nuncio amiably recalled this weakness to the French themselves, referring to an incident that had occurred in 1922 at the time of the election of Pius XI. He himself had been on St. Peter's Square waiting for the wisps of smoke from the chimney of the Sistine Chapel. When it became white and the senior Cardinal Deacon announced, amid the joy of the crowd, that Cardinal Achille Ratti, Archbishop of Milan, had been elected, for the first time since 1870 a Pope appeared to bless the crowds from an outside balcony of the basilica.

The Nuncio was standing near a group of French seminarians who seemed to be perplexed by the event. Finally one of them screwed up his courage and asked him:

"Does he love France?"

"*Mais bien sûr!*"

After receiving this assurance from Mons. Roncalli

the young theologians of the seminary of Santa Chiara joined without reserve in the celebration going on about them and warmly applauded the new Pontiff.

In no case was Mons. Roncalli ever discourteous. Shortly before the 1951 elections an article on the French situation which was published in Rome had given rise to many protests, especially in circles favorable to General De Gaulle. Around that time the Nuncio participated in a ceremony at the Hôtel de Ville in Paris and the President of the municipal council, Pierre De Gaulle, a brother of the General, made some rather obvious allusions to the article (which had wrongly been attributed to Vatican inspiration), and expressed hope for a different attitude on the part of the Holy See. The Nuncio, who was also one of the speakers, proceeded to make some observations on the millennial anniversary of Paris which was being celebrated. Then among other things he said that he had visited an exhibit of old and rare books and that he had noted with great pleasure that the first Italian book to be published in France, five centuries before, was a work on politeness and good manners by one who was almost his fellow townsman, a certain Gasperino da Barzizza.

The French press, especially the non-Gaullist, chose to interpret the Nuncio's words as a reply to Pierre De Gaulle's inopportune remarks. Mons. Roncalli, however, has always denied that the reference to Gasperino was intentional. If one does not accept his words at face value, then one does not know him.

It is opportune to recall this particular incident here because many newspapers mentioned it following the election of John XXIII. Perhaps some future biographer may take note of it. The only fact this story brings out is a deliberately misleading interpretation of a little speech made for a special occasion.

Mons. Roncalli was generous toward all, even his adversaries. The former Minister of Foreign Affairs of France and author of the Schuman Plan for Europe, recently recalled a significant episode: "Just before leaving France, Mons. Roncalli, the future Pope, was attacked on the floor of the National Assembly by a deputy who, indeed, was more incongruous than malicious. I was then Secretary of Foreign Affairs and it became my honor to defend the Nuncio for the Government. The next day, Mons. Roncalli said to me, 'Thank you for your speech, but I thank you especially for not having said something which could hurt that deputy.'"

During his period of service in Paris, Monsignor Roncalli also served for nineteen months as the first permanent observer of the Holy See with UNESCO, one of the ten specialized agencies affiliated with the United Nations, and having as its purpose to contribute to world peace by collaboration among nations through education, science and culture. Everyone in the cultural organization of the United Nations on Rue Kléber remembers his visits and his speeches at the general conferences, his homilies at the Masses which preceded the opening of the sessions. He always had a sympathetic word for each and every one, singularly appropriate to their nationality and duties. He wished to know everybody from the highest functionary to the least clerk, and if there was time, he would stop to talk with each one, asking questions about his work, his country and his family.

The speech that the permanent observer for the Holy See delivered in July 1951 at the sixth general conference is memorable. In reality it was a warning to the organization not to go beyond certain limits, but it was couched in such a way that it seemed to be a eulogy, and it showed a profound grasp of the problems facing the organization.

"UNESCO," he said in part, "no longer seems to be what one might have feared it was at the beginning, that is, a grand museum dedicated to the intellectual distraction of the culture of a curious throng. Instead it is a great and blazing hearth whose sparks will everywhere arouse energetic efforts and a vast cooperation on behalf of justice, freedom and peace for all peoples without distinction of race, language or religion.

"Yes, without distinction of race, language or religion. If I underline this clear position of UNESCO, contained in its constitution, it is not because the racial, literary or religious values of different peoples are being ignored or neglected, but rather so that these values may always be held in the highest esteem. UNESCO . . . must be neither blind nor deaf to the fundamental . . . psychology of each people, that is, to its national sense and its religious spirit. Such are the proofs of UNESCO's good-will in the face of situations and fundamental problems, an attitude which assures the trust and collaboration of the greatest part of mankind in this great international organization. . . ."

This was said at a time when certain signs gave rise to the fear that UNESCO would become the promoter of a standardized culture, a "super-ministry of education" that would suffocate the traditions and values of different peoples, and would superimpose on single groups a kind of religious syncretism that by degrees was supposed to descend from on high to those below. Mons. Roncalli was warning the organization to avoid errors of this kind.

Undoubtedly a flair for diplomacy is a natural gift, but to this endowment Nuncio Roncalli added gifts acquired by a long study of the human heart. It must not be thought that his friendships were diplomatic so to speak, that is, not of a disinterested character. He loves people for themselves and never forgets that he is a priest.

Everybody in Paris knew that Nuncio Roncalli had a particular sympathy for Edouard Herriot, ex-President of the Council who was then living out the last years of his life. Herriot had always been—and still was —the most authoritative representative of the Radical Party and a high dignitary of French Masonry which, in contrast to Anglo-Saxon Masonry, is violently anti-Catholic. But he was appreciative of the Nuncio's friendship and responded to it no less warmly. He knew that Mons. Roncalli prayed for him and, although he smiled over the idea of anybody praying for him, he was grateful. Only God can say what part this cordial and disinterested friendship played in the drama that unfolded at the bedside of the dying Herriot when the lifelong anti-clerical accepted the absolution imparted to him in *articulo mortis* by Cardinal Gerlier, Archbishop of Lyons.

Even though he was an able diplomat, His Excellency the Most Reverend Mons. Angelo Roncalli, titular Archbishop of Mesembria and Apostolic Nuncio, did not for this reason cease to be a man of God, even for a moment. We can see only the external reflections of his intense life of piety, known only to a few intimates, in the form of his prayers, charities and the amiability of his conduct toward all. He held the Virgin of Lourdes in devout veneration and his stay in France enabled him to make frequent visits to the grotto at Massabielle, thus continuing the pilgrimages he had begun long ago in 1905 as the youthful and timid secretary of Mons. Radini-Tedeschi.

During the period of his nunciature in Paris, Mons. Roncalli visited the banks of the Gave almost every year. In 1947 he presided over the French national pilgrimage, the spiritual aim of which was "to pray for peace in the world." On that occasion the Nuncio accepted the title of honorary canon of the Cathedral of Tarbes. And during the 1954 Marian year, Cardinal Roncalli, already Patriarch of Venice, accompanied by all the bishops of the Venetian Province, led a large regional pilgrimage to Lourdes.

On March 25, 1958, when he returned to Lourdes to consecrate the great underground basilica, constructed on the occasion of the miraculous grotto's centenary, he told the prefect of the Hautes Pyrénées who welcomed him at the Ossun airport that he could be considered one of the oldest pilgrims to the Grotto of Massa-bielle. In his homily delivered during the first Mass celebrated in the subterranean church, he exalted the Marian devotion of France which, rising from the crypt of Chartres to the sublimity of the heights of La Salette, now returned to find expression in underground Lourdes in the largest church in the world except for the Basilica of St. Peter.

Almost as though he were praying, he said, "She is always there, venerable and pious brethren. She is always there in the act of fulfilling her pious mission. Mary is here, as she is in the grotto, the crypt, as she is in the higher and lower basilicas; she is always there, the Mother of Jesus and our Mother. Always is she there, ever in the act of carrying out her maternal mission, the mission proclaimed by her son Jesus. She listens, enlightens, consoles, heals, and encourages all those who appeal to her. . . ."

Before entering the papal conclave, Cardinal Roncalli wrote to the Bishop of Lourdes: "At the moment of entering the conclave my thoughts bring me back to Lourdes, to the Basilica of St. Pius X and, above all, to the Immaculate Virgin of the Grotto."

During his stay in France, apart from his frequent returns to Lourdes, he was present at all the most important Marian celebrations. He was in La Salette in 1946, on the centenary of the apparition when the fifth National Marian Congress was held in that celebrated sanctuary. On this occasion he expressed the hope that the diplomats then gathered in Paris would forget their secondary differences and establish peace in the true spiritual climate which alone could assure its permanence. He was at Rennes in 1950, and in his frequent travels throughout France he visited and revisited all the famous French sanctuaries one by one, and often stopped in the most humble and remote churches for prayer and meditation.

As is known, the Apostolic Nuncio to France was elevated to the rank of cardinal by Pius XII at the consistory of January 12, 1953. It is not so well known that he received his cardinal's red biretta, brought to Paris by a papal ablegate and a member of the Noble Guard, from the hands of the President of the French Republic, Vincent Auriol.

On the basis of ancient privileges accorded to the sovereigns of certain countries, newly appointed cardinals residing outside Rome receive the biretta from the head of the State. This is the custom in Spain, Portugal and Austria. France also enjoyed this privilege until the separation between France and the Holy See which took place at the beginning of the twentieth century; the last ceremony of this kind had taken place in Paris on May 29, 1897. Following the resumption of diplomatic relations between France and the Holy See this privilege was restored and the nuncios were again to receive the red biretta from the hands of the head of the State.

President Auriol, an old Socialist, sincerely liked Nuncio Roncalli but he was rather embarrassed by the prospect of the ceremony. A convinced secularist, it seemed to him that the result of presenting a biretta to a Roman cardinal would be to compromise certain rigid principles which the Fourth Republic had inherited from the Third. Thus he wanted the ceremony to be conducted as inconspicuously as possible in the presence of the President of the Council, Mayer; the Minister of Foreign Affairs, Bidault; and the ambassadors of Canada, Turkey and Italy. The Canadian had expressed the wish to be present because of his status as vice-dean of the diplomatic corps, and the Turkish ambassador wanted to attend in memory of Mons. Roncalli's mission to Istanbul. The Italian ambassador, of course, asked to be invited as the representative of the native country of the new cardinal. The Nuncio, however, after direct negotiations with the mistress of the household, Madame Auriol, requested and obtained permission to invite some friends and acquaintances. As a result, the mayor of Bergamo, the parish priest of Sotto il Monte, and a group of fellow townsmen came to Paris.

There was something quite extraordinary about this gathering: the guests ranged in rank from the highest functionaires of the French Republic to humble inhabitants of little villages of Val Brembana. A dash of color was provided by the prelatial robes of the ablegate, Mons. Giacomo Testa, the present apostolic delegate to Istanbul, and by the escort of the Noble Guard. All the others were dressed in irreproachable black, an achievement in itself since some unknown persons had walked away with the suitcases of the Cardinal's friends from Bergamo at the moment of their arrival at the Paris nunciature. These suitcases contained their formal evening wear and the guests from Bergamo had to scurry about frantically for new dress suits so as not to cut a poor figure at the ceremony honoring their most eminent fellow townsman.

The ceremony was a brief one. In presenting Nuncio Roncalli with the biretta President Auriol said:

"The French Government has been deeply sensible of your constant cordiality and of the concern which you have shown for all generous undertakings and for all works of peace, in accordance with the noble and paternal teaching of the Supreme Head of the Church. And I myself, Monsieur le Cardinal, recall our conversations on the first of January with a particular emotion. Your messages will remain for everyone as examples of wisdom, refinement and friendship. The regret that the imminent departure of Your Eminence occasions us, and which is shared by your eminent colleagues of the diplomatic corps, is tempered by the joy that we feel in seeing a Prince of the Church, a great connoisseur of things French, number us, as you have just declared, among your certain and sincere friends. . . ."

Later President Auriol decorated the Cardinal with the medal of the Grand Cross of the Legion of Honor, the highest French award.

The Nuncio, visibly moved, replied. "It will be enough if every Frenchman, recalling my humble name and my sojourn among you, will be able to say: he was a loyal and peaceful priest." These were the last words he spoke publicly in France.

After a stay of eight years Angelo Giuseppe Roncalli left France as a Cardinal of the Holy Roman Church. His role as a diplomat had come to an end, and his role as a shepherd of souls was beginning.

Before leaving, however, he gathered around his table all those political leaders who during his stay in Paris had been Presidents of the Council of Ministers. Among them were MM. Herriot, Bidault, Schuman, Mayer, Sarraut and many others. And they were all his friends; even those far removed from the Catholic faith and from religion in general came to say farewell with sincere affection to a man who had dealt sincerely with them when they were the rulers of France, in order to protect the welfare of the Church and of the Holy See and the prerogatives of the Christian conscience.

Following his election to the Papacy, French newspapers recalled that the Nuncio's attitudes were not always understood by those who because of congenital factionalism are accustomed to judge people on the basis of their "choices." "Progressivism" and "integralism" were two words and concepts which made laborious entry into Mons. Roncalli's thinking; his thoughts were rather turned to unity and to avoiding the dangers of divisiveness.[5]

The Nuncio left Paris leaving behind many friends and not a single enemy. M. de la Chauvinière, chief of protocol of the French Ministry of Foreign Affairs, declared upon the election of the former Nuncio to the Papacy: "On all official occasions and even more in our private talks I was able to appreciate the fineness of his mind, the generosity of his feelings and his very great sense of tolerance. I enjoyed the witty or gracious allusions in his talks, but above all I observed his great love for France and his interest in everything which bore on the preservation of peace."

[5] *Informations Catholiques Internationales*, Paris, 15, XI, 58. n.54.

M. de la Chauvinière's predecessor at the Quai d'Orsay, M. Jacques Domaine in his published memoirs recalled his first meeting with Mons. Roncalli and the words with which the Nuncio sought to express the nature of his mission to France. "My role in France," murmured Mons. Roncalli as he adjusted his *zucchetto*, "is that of St. Joseph: to be a guardian over Our Lord and to protect Him with discretion."

VI

The Patriarch of Venice

Pax Tibi Marce

CARDINAL RONCALLI made a triumphal entry into his patriarchal city of Venice on March 15, 1953, having started out on his journey from the episcopal palace of Padua. He later recalled that as he took his first steps in his new diocese he looked out over the lagoon where the land and sea seemed loath to part from one another because the old, melancholy islands, so rich in history and artistic treasures, form a shelter against the pounding waves of the Adriatic. It was from this moment that he began to know this city, born from the sea, and its kindly inhabitants. This was the starting point of his pastoral ministry.

In Paris two months before, the Cardinal, as was his custom, had been scanning the newspapers when his eyes fell on a photo published by the newspaper *Figaro* over the caption, "The Gondola of Death." It was the funeral gondola that had transported the Venetian Patriarch Mons. Agostini to the cemetery of San Michele in Isola. Mons. Agostini had himself been elevated to the purple but he had died on December 28, 1952, before he could receive his red hat. Angelo Giuseppe Roncalli was pensive as he looked at the photograph, then cut it out and placed it in his breviary as a marker. When Mons. Agostini was still living Archbishop Roncalli had received a confidential communication to the effect that the Holy Father intended sending him to Venice whenever that post should become vacant.

Now he was entering his see city. The embankments and their connecting passages, the open squares, the ramps of the three bridges thrown across the Grand Canal were thronged with people; rich tapestries had been hung from the windows of the ancient palaces along the waterway. The motor launch of the Admiralty, carrying the Cardinal on board, proceeded majestically down the canal, followed by the flotilla of gaily adorned gondolas. The good people of Venice applauded joyously as the Patriarch, with tears in his eyes, raised his hand in blessing.

More than forty years before, on November 24, 1894, Giuseppe Cardinal Sarto had also entered the city as its Patriarch. The Venetians themselves had accorded a memorable welcome to the future St. Pius X, but no sound had come from the municipal building, the shutters of its windows ostentatiously closed. The city administration at that time wished to ignore the entry of the Patriarch.

"We will open those windows again," Pius X had remarked sadly on that occasion.

Since that time, for forty years no Patriarch had entered the city as a Cardinal: the former patriarchs, Cavallari, La Fontaine, and Piazza had received their red hats after they had already been installed for some time in their see.

The new pastor wore the Roman purple and not the robe of "patriarchal" color, which is something between violet and red and which the "Most Serene Republic," no stranger to long-drawn-out disputes with the Holy See, had imposed on its Patriarchs, perhaps to make them quasi-cardinals *motu proprio*. This time the civic authorities, led by the Mayor, all were present. Reverent and deeply moved, they tendered the Patriarch a welcome with all the honors due his rank and office.

The cortege, gliding along the Grand Canal in a sea of color, arrived at the quay of St. Mark amid the applause of the crowd, at that point where the lagoon widens and is separated from the open sea only by the thin, insular strip of the Lido, looming gray and low in the distance. The motor launch hauled alongside the dock of the square and the Cardinal disembarked, blessing the throng. He kissed the crucifix, and after acknowledging the Mayor's speech of welcome he made his way toward the Basilica of St. Mark, glittering with gold like a precious treasure box offered to God in propitiation. At the entrance he turned around again to bless the crowd on the balconies and around the buildings of the square, in the shadow of the tall bell tower of St. Mark's. Immediately upon entering the church, he mounted the pulpit from which he delivered his first address to the people of Venice:

"*Ecce homo, ecce sacerdos, ecce pastor* (Behold the man, the priest, the pastor).

"I wish to speak to you with the utmost frankness of heart and language. You have been awaiting me anxiously, and things have been written and said about me which go beyond my merits. Humbly I now present myself.

"I am like every other man who lives in the world. I have been endowed with the grace of good physical health, with a little good sense that enables me to look quickly and clearly into the heart of things, and with a disposition to love mankind which keeps me faithful to the injunctions of the Gospel, respectful of my rights and those of others and which prevents me from doing evil to anyone. Indeed, it encourages me to do good to all.

"I come from humble beginnings, and I was raised in a restraining, blessed poverty, whose needs are few and which protects the growth of the highest and noblest virtues and prepares one for the great ascents of life. Providence took me away from my native village and led me to travel the roads of the world in the East and in the West, bringing me in touch with peoples of different religions and ideologies, and in contact with acute and threatening social problems. Yet, safeguarded by my loyalty to the principles of Catholic belief and morality, I have tried to preserve my calm and balance while investigating and evaluating things and persons about me, ever concerned more with that which unites than with that which divides and gives rise to differences.

"These brief words trace the modest physiognomy

of the man before you. To be sure the position that has been entrusted to me in Venice is a great one and surpasses my every merit. But before all else I recommend to your benevolence a man who above all else wishes simply to be your loving brother, approachable and understanding. . . ."

"Such is the man, such is the new citizen whom Venice has been pleased to welcome so festively.

"The priest: *ecce sacerdos*. Ever since I was born I thought of nothing else save to become a priest. Thus was the humble son of the people installed in the divine office for the benefit of the people in the things which are God's: as the representative of the people in a daily offering of gifts and sacrifices to the Lord, in a ministry of propitiation for sins and sinners, in a constant act of offering. . . .

"As you look at your Patriarch, look for the priest, the minister of grace and look for naught else, because he wishes to translate into his ministry this vocation given to him by God. Consequently, his activity would be priestly.

"Shepherd, *ecce pastor*. A little man, a humble priest, but above all a shepherd. . . .

"Jesus is the Eternal Shepherd of our souls and the model of the pastoral office: *Pastor et episcopus animarum nostrarum*. The Pope is the Universal Shepherd and around and with him are the Bishops, and among them is your Patriarch.

"From the beginning of my clerical life, I aspired only to become a country priest in my diocese. But Providence has wished to send me along other paths.

However, in the many missions entrusted to me by
Holy Church, and in my contacts with peoples of different religions and races, it has always been my constant care to bring forth the pastoral note and with this
I am content.

"The triumphal procession that you have prepared
for me shows what the Patriarch means to Venetians.
These kindly glances, these smiling faces, these delicate
attentions have revealed to me your goodness and your
communion with my spirit.

"I will return the kindness of your gift of welcome
to me today. I will quickly and rapidly be in touch with
you all, but in a simple not in a solemn way, and in the
manner of the shepherd who counts his sheep one by
one.

"Thus will be my ministry among you. Do not look
upon your Patriarch as a man of politics, as a diplomat.
Look for the shepherd of souls, who exercises his office
among you in the name of Our Lord. The pastor goes
ahead of all others; he opens the gate and leads his flock
to green pastures; he gives up his life for his flock.

"My work here will depend on the precious cooperation of the ecclesiastical and civil authorities. Today
I have seen an example of the edifying unity between
these two orders in Venice. And I have also seen the
unity of the clergy, both secular and regular, who, root-
ing themselves in eternal principles, wish to cooperate
for the good of the Christian people.

"I place my ministry under the protection of the Ni-
copeia Madonna whom you so greatly venerate, and

who from now on will receive the confidences of the new Patriarch as she did those of his predecessors.

"May the protecting Saints of this illustrious see assist me!"

The Patriarch then closed his address, which had deeply moved his hearers, with an ardent invocation to his predecessor St. Pius X.

Angelo Cardinal Roncalli, titular priest of the Roman Church of Saint Prisca and the new Patriarch of Venice, had not attended the consistory of January 12, 1953, because, as we have seen, he was in Paris. The petitioning for and the laying on of the *pallium*—the white stole bordered with black crosses which symbolizes the jurisdiction of metropolitan archbishops—had taken place by proxy. The *pallium* had been received for him by Cardinal Piazza from the hands of Cardinal Tisserant, the delegate of the Holy Father, on the morning of January 15 in the Pauline Chapel of the Vatican. With this ceremony Angelo Roncalli had become the forty-fourth Patriarch and the one hundred thirty-ninth Ordinary of the see of Venice.

He arrived in Rome, directly from Paris, on the first day of March. On March 5, in accordance with the regulations of the concordat between Italy and the Holy See, he took the oath of loyalty to the Italian government required of bishops of Italian sees and administered by the President of the Republic who was then Senator Luigi Einaudi.

By rule the oath should have been preceded by the presentation of the *galero*, the big pontifical red hat which the cardinals of the Holy Roman Church receive from the hands of the Pope and which they never wear: it is placed on their coffins when they die and is hung from the ceiling of their cathedral after their burial. But Pius XII was indisposed on that day and by a special dispensation he permitted the Patriarch to take the oath before the presentation of the cardinal's ring and the red hat so as not to delay his entry to a diocese awaiting his arrival. The ceremony took place later, on October 20th, in Castelgandolfo.

As we have seen, the shepherd presented himself to his flock with the sincere humility of one who has watched his words and actions all his life with the firm intention of truly being a father and brother to men.

The Patriarch of Venice also functions as the metropolitan of the province of Veneto for the dioceses of Adria, Feltre-Belluno, Chioggia, Concordia, Padua, Treviso, Verona, Vicenza, and Vittorio Veneto. In addition he is president of the Tri-Venetian Episcopal Conference which, in addition to the bishops of the aforementioned dioceses, includes the archbishops of Udine, Trento, and the bishops of Bresanone, Gorizia, Gradisca and Trieste-Capodistria.

This is an honorary primacy but on certain important occasions the good sense and the experience of the metropolitan may have a great influence on the entire ecclesiastical province. But without neglecting these duties, the Patriarch from the very first day dedicated himself heart and soul to his pastoral ministry. For this aspect of his activity we now turn to one who was very close to him in those years as his secretary, Mons. Loris

Capovilla. Mons. Capovilla has followed Cardinal Roncalli to Rome and he has remained close to John XXIII,
refusing every honor that has been offered to him because he is content to remain Roncalli's secretary just as
he was in Venice. This is how Mons. Capovilla has described the Patriarch's day:

". . . The arduous day began (and begins) early in
the morning at 4 A.M. Prayer, the breviary, spiritual
reading; at 7 A.M. Holy Mass; at 8 A.M. a cup of milk
and some fruit. Then the correspondence and other office matters are attended to, followed by a rapid perusal
of the newspapers in which nothing of importance es-
capes his attention because items of interest are underlined. Callers were received from 10 A.M. to 1 P.M.
After lunch a visit to the chapel for prayer before the
Blessed Sacrament, followed by a half-hour rest period
and then a return to work, resumed calmly, methodi-
cally, and during which the problems of the morning
were studied more thoroughly. In the afternoon he presided at meetings of diocesan committees or received
visitors who came to see him about diocesan or curial
affairs. At 7:45 P.M. recitation of the rosary in the
chapel with the members of his household. The third
mysteries of the rosary were usually recited in unison,
but he would recite the other two parts alone. Then, at
8 P.M., supper, followed by a brief pause in his study.
Finally, he would retire at 10 P.M."

Although this was his usual schedule, according to
Mons. Capovilla it was not rigid or immutably fixed. In
fact, it was broken very often for reasons connected
with his pastorate or his studies.

"Sometimes the Patriarch would remain in his library without interruption from 9 P.M. to 4 A.M. in order to prepare a pastoral letter, a speech, or in order to study some book thoroughly. On such occasions he only rested between 4 A.M. and 7:30 A.M. At other times he retired even before 9 P.M., but then he would get up again at 1 A.M. for his prayers, and for any reading or study that was most urgent. He never missed attending the annual spiritual exercises together with the entire episcopate of the Venetian province. This tradition which had been established by Cardinal La Fontaine was continued by the new Patriarch with a pious fervor, just as he never failed to attend the monthly retreats and study-gatherings of his clergy with edifying and exemplary piety. His favorite reading: Holy Scripture, the Church Fathers, the great French orators, the Spanish mystics, church history, the lives of the saints, books on the liturgy and on pastoral problems, historical researches.

He especially liked to invite prelates of the Church to the Patriarchate for the celebration of sacred rites. Thus he arranged for the panegyric to St. Mark to be delivered each year by a Venetian bishop. Eminent dignitaries of the Church came to Venice to celebrate pontifical masses there and to deliver addresses: Cardinals Lercaro, Agagianian, Feltin, Gilroy, Costantini and others . . ." [1]

Such a routine might appear to be that of a pious and

[1] Published anonymously in the *Osservatore Romano*, October 30, 1958.

learned prelate immersed in prayer and study, but not of one close to his flock. But by now we are already sufficiently familiar with the character of Angelo Giuseppe Roncalli to know that he is not prone to isolation nor does he approve it. As a matter of fact, Mons. Loris Capovilla continues:

"In the five years of his pastorate he made more than one visit to each of his parishes. He celebrated Mass in each one at an early hour and later preached at later Masses, often four and six times during the day. At San Lorenzo in Mestre he gave ten sermons in one day. He took special interest in parish archives and records. He would converse with the little children in the catechism classes so that they would not hold their Bishop in awe and fear. His very criticism of his priests, when this was necessary, was a source of comfort to them because of the delicacy, amiability and respect in which it was couched. Above all, he was so tactful in this that neither the laity nor even the members of the priests' household ever became aware of the criticism. He would often go into the kitchens to thank the humble women who took care of the rectories, displaying a quality of goodness he had in common with St. Pius X. At table his conversational tone was friendly, informal and light in tone, concentrating on no special subject. In the afternoon he visited the sick and presided at the meetings of parochial councils. He wanted to be informed about all the activities going on in the parish, and interested himself in churches, chapels and other consecrated buildings both from a liturgical and a historical point of view.

Finally vespers were a great source of enjoyment to him when they were sung by the faithful attending the services. . . .

"In Venice proper and throughout the archdiocese it was customary for him to visit religious hospitals and institutions. He called a diocesan synod from November 24 to 27 in 1957, and in 1954 he sponsored very solemn religious celebrations in honor of the Marian centenary. He was the organizing spirit behind the great pilgrimage to Lourdes of Venetian bishops. And in 1955, as the Apostolic Legate to the Marian Congress in Beirut, he crowned the statue of Our Lady in Lebanon."

Mons. Loris Capovilla then concludes his reminiscences of Cardinal Roncalli with an account of his achievements in the city of which he was Patriarch:

". . . he built the minor seminary, thirty new parishes, invited the order of the sons of St. Jerome Miani to settle in Mestre, and entrusted to them the sanctuary of the Immaculate Heart of Mary. He reorganized the houses of the canons around the seat of the Patriarchate. His improvements increased the splendor of the basilica of St. Mark, and it was at his wish that the remains of his predecessors were placed in the crypt close to the relics of St. Mark. He acquired the historic San Giorgio in Alga. He also established a new center for the archives of the patriarchate. . . .

"He devoted his careful attention to Catholic Action as the indispensable modern apostolate of the Church. And he was present at all the social, cultural and recreational gatherings of Catholic Action groups, encouraging and inspiring them with his words. Often this interest in Catholic Action took him beyond the city of Venice. For example, he was at the Eucharistic or Marian Congresses in Turin in 1953, in Lecce 1957, Padua in 1954, and 1958, Belluno 1956, Vicenza 1957, Verona 1958, Faenza (September 14, 1958), Palermo (September 1957 during the Pro-Orient Week), and in Lodi on the occasion of the eight hundredth anniversary of the reconstructed city."

Venice is one of the Italian cities which enjoys an intense national and international cultural life. In this connection it is enough to recall the biennial exposition of the plastic arts, the film exhibitions and the music festivals. The center of the island of San Giorgio Maggiore (which contains the abbey where was held the conclave that elected Pius VII at the end of the eighteenth century) is the site of many cultural exhibits and congresses of all kinds. To this, of course, must be added the influx of tourists who come either to see the artistic and panoramic marvels of the "Pearl of the Adriatic" or to enjoy the gay social life of the celebrated Lido beach.

It was not unusual, therefore, for many of these gatherings to be clouded by incidents which could hardly be approved, to say the least, from a moral viewpoint. In the summertime the poor guard in his picturesque uniform stationed at the entrance to the basilica of St. Mark's had to work hard to keep foreigners, coming from or going to the Lido, away from a place of worship which they thought they could visit in beach costumes that were more than scanty.

The Patriarch Cardinal Roncalli observed these excesses and he condemned them with the humorous sense of moderation so characteristic of him. This is how he expressed himself regarding certain over-abbreviated styles of feminine dress.

". . . People don't have to come to Italy wrapped in furs. But Italy is not exactly below the Equator. And even down there, for that matter, lions wear their coats and crocodiles are protected by their precious skins. . . ."

Generally at the opening of the biennial art exhibition, his predecessors had forbidden the clergy to visit it because they did not consider it proper or fitting for priests or religious to view statues, paintings and prints with subject matter that was morally decadent, even for the laudable purpose of familiarizing themselves with the loftier expressions of modern art.

Patriarch Roncalli, however, amazed everyone and even scandalized some timid souls by himself visiting the biennial exhibit. True, he avoided the rooms containing works of an excessively free character, but by his presence he wished to make it known that he considered art *per se* as a noble human activity and experience to which the Church is not alien. Who does not know that art, after centuries of darkness, received its baptism from the Church and came to the fullness of its maturity in the temples of Christianity? The improper use that many make of artistic expression, the very appeal to art in order to justify immoral creations, cannot belie this fact. The secret lies in guiding art back to a healthier source of inspiration. This cannot be done by running away from artists but by approaching them so that they may understand that their gifts do not place them beyond good and evil, indeed that their very gifts make them all the more responsible.

This was true also of the cinema. Cardinal Roncalli never visited the Film Festival but when he addressed the actors and directors during the special Masses said for them he exhorted them to give a Christian and human dignity to their works of art. On August 31, 1958, he declared:

"The Church considers all expressions of human activity with a sense both of reserve and trust. She followed the first steps of the cinema and judged them with benevolence and, ever patient and far-seeing, has expressed the hope that the 'week of the arts,' as it is called, will be productive of good results.

"The impression created by a film can arise either under the influence of a mind that disciplines and directs the feelings and passions, or else under the overwhelming and disordered drives of those forces which, unleashed, have never failed to leave ruin, desolation, tears and blood in their wake . . .

"May you in your efforts and concern to better film production and to disseminate it through the world always be inspired by what is noble and just, useful and good for everybody, for children, young people and adults. It is a fact that for at least one hour a week the greater part of mankind entrusts itself to you—I was about to say almost totally and childishly—in happy and pleasurable expectation of a bit of illusion, understood as such, and of a portrayal of those feelings which soften the soul and bring it true recreation."

This is a fitting place to point out that Angelo Giuseppe Roncalli is a man of articulate taste and that he is not a stranger to the experiments and expressions of modern art. If his humanistic inclinations lead him to prefer the great works of the past this does not mean that he ignores the present. Journalists who visited the patriarchal palace in Venice immediately after his election were surprised to find the poems of Rimbaud and *The Diary of a Country Priest* by Bernanos in the Cardinal's library. An alert feeling for beauty and an innate respect for man and his manifestations combine to make him an uncynical observer of the insights and experiments of modern art. Although he rejects its more flagrant abuses, he is prepared to perceive those qualities in modern works of art which endow them with an enduring value.

When he arrived in Venice the people spoke of him as "the calm after the storm." According to these merry gossips, the storm was supposed to have been his predecessor, the very strict Patriarch Agostini who had been most austere in his demands upon his priests and faithful. The calm, of course, was Cardinal Roncalli because of his placid and serene appearance, the ease with which he approached people, the informality of his conversation with everyone, the benign quality of his judgments, and his indulgence toward all in every circumstance. In short an "easy-going" priest.

For a time it looked as if this were really so. But gradually it became clear to all that the "calm" of the new Patriarch had the same objectives as Mons. Agostini had set for himself. Their methods were radically different, but Cardinal Roncalli worked in a more direct and paternal way for the sanctification of his flock. He moved among his faithful to support and comfort them with his presence. It was not long before his people began to love him.

The Patriarch never left his residence without a definite destination. One day, accompanied by the faithful Don Capovilla, he wanted to visit the city's parks. After his tour he felt too tired to walk the long way back to his residence, so he took the *vaporetto*, seating himself among the boat's passengers. He was immediately recognized and some of those on board wanted to kiss his ring. The Patriarch began to talk with his fellow passengers, and they all gathered around him happily, surprised at finding how easy it was to talk with him. When the motorboat hauled alongside the quay at St. Mark's many of the passengers walked along with him in order that they might continue their conversation.

Anecdotes about the Patriarch began to circulate just as they had in the time of Pius X. One day his secretary had given a mendicant a hundred lire; the Patriarch pointed out that to be really helpful he should have given him at least a thousand lire, in view of the inflation. Another story concerns a very fat person who was struggling hard to catch up with the Cardinal because he wanted to talk with him. The Patriarch turned around and said, "The Lord must certainly have patience with us fat people."

These anecdotes—true or invented—continue to multiply and it may well happen that in the confusion of time stories that really involved Giuseppe Sarto will be attributed to Angelo Roncalli.

His Parisian friends were frequent visitors to Venice. Cardinal Feltin tells the story that during his journey to Venice—it was the feast day of St. Mark—the Patriarch took a stroll with him to St. Mark's Square where a band concert was being given. Going up to the conductor, the Patriarch requested him to play the *Marseillaise* in honor of his guest. The maestro and his band obliged, to the great applause of the crowd.

Once Vincent Auriol came to Venice, no longer the President of the French Republic but an ordinary citizen. When the Patriarch heard that his friend was in the city he quickly went to visit him at his hotel and embraced him in the lobby in the presence of everybody there. "Then," Auriol said later, "I went to the Patriarchate and he showed me a modest room sparingly furnished, and said to me, 'This is where Pius X lived.' In turn I replied, 'Perhaps the successor to Pius XII will also leave from here.' He smiled but did not answer. . . ."

The French writers, François Mauriac and Wladimir d'Ormesson, also came to Venice and enjoyed the warm and cordial hospitality of their friend the Patriarch.

The clergy of Venice remember him with special affection. According to the older canons of St. Mark's, "The Patriarch brought us back in memory to the days of Cardinal La Fontaine and Giuseppe Sarto because his last predecessors, Cardinal Piazza and Mons. Agostini, were good-hearted men but austere in manner and bearing."

During his visits to the old parishes of the city as well as to the new ones which had come into being as the result of his efforts, the Patriarch gave careful attention to the most minute detail, but he was never severe with anyone. He merely said whatever had to be said. "He was a father," a young curate once observed, "not a policeman." Whenever something did displease him his severest reprimand was to say, "Such things happen when little boys are in charge."

We will recall that during Mons. Angelo Roncalli's nunciature in Paris, there was a big question among Catholic circles involved in politics, or in those issues that stand midway between morality and politics, of whether the Pope's representative was a "religious" or a "political" man, an "integralist" or one whose mind was opening to daring ideas inspired by the generous idealism of youth. It was a question to which they were unable to find an answer until they realized that the nuncio was above all a shepherd of souls, a true pastor. Receptive as he was to everything and everybody, he never for a moment permitted anything that was detrimental to the doctrines or discipline of the Church, no matter how good the intention. It was in such situations that his gift of charitableness came to the fore and was most effectively displayed.

He maintained this same attitude in Venice where, however, he did not fail to take steps to clear up misunderstandings that endangered souls.

Venice was and still is the center of a left-wing group within the Christian Democratic Party. This group which defines itself as a "Leftist Base" published a weekly called *Il Popolo Veneto*. The young people behind this movement came from the Catholic Action organization, more exactly from the Youth Group within Catholic Action, and the affair reflected an internal crisis within the organization which occasioned much discussion in Italy at that time. In reality, the crisis had deeper roots; it had begun with the transformation—imperceptible but real—undergone by Italian Catholic Action in those years.

Catholic Action, in so far as it involves the cooperation of the laity with the hierarchy, is a movement for the religious education and apostolic action of this laity. It is supposed to concern itself with deepening the Catholic religious consciousness of its own members, with bringing back those who have strayed or fallen away from the Faith, and at the same time with preparing men to bear open witness to Christ. It is therefore alien to any party politics whatsoever. However, in view of the situation existing in Italy for the past fifteen years, and in view of the existence of a Catholic political party which moreover was one in power, it was not always easy for Catholic Action to keep free of attitudes which if not political attitudes proper were at least akin to them. Clearly Catholics are united and in agreement on the religious terrain, but in the arena of politics everyone can have an individual opinion, and differences of opinion can arise and often these differences come to the surface.

It should occasion no surprise then that a certain political turn, more accidental than designed, infiltrated Italian Catholic Action where rightist tendencies were counterpoised by tendencies that were or seemed to be leftist. It is clear, after what we have said, that the blame for this should be equally shared by both sides.

The Italian "Right" is a conglomeration of states of mind, so to speak, which does not stress an ideology as such, while the Italian "Left" is composed of Communists and Socialists, that is, of political parties whose world views are materialistic and in every case incompatible with the Catholic religion.

It was to be expected, therefore, that the leftist orientation of the young people in Catholic Action would occasion more serious apprehensions and misgivings than the opposite tendency. Dr. Mario Rossi, the president general of the Catholic Action Youth resigned—to all intents and purposes he was removed—for having adopted leftist political attitudes bordering on philosocialism, and a group of his young friends broke with the organization.

These young men continued their activity on a political rather than a religious terrain within the Christian Democratic Party. One of the most active centers of their movement was a region of Venice and in particular the city of Venice, where, as has been said, the weekly *Il Popolo Veneto* was published. Following the twentieth congress of the Russian Communist Party, the young people connected with *Il Popolo Veneto* began to speak and to write about the possibilities of cooperating with the Socialists whether or not these adhered to their so-called "pact of unity" with the Communist Party which, they believed, had changed its character. It was a commonly shared illusion, in fact, that the twentieth Bolshevik Congress had marked a break with the old Communist methods and the beginning of an authentic democratization of Soviet society. The Hungarians had to pay a very high price for this illusion and in the U.S.S.R. it found its most dramatic expression in the case of the writer Pasternak, who translated these "hopes" in his book *Doctor Zhivago*.

The Venetian episode, in itself unimportant, had great reverberations in Italy because there arose a tendency to judge the entire Christian Democratic Party on the basis of this small leftist group. If this party, which for years had been the most solid bulwark against Communism, "opened itself to the Left" how would things end?

Cardinal Roncalli, perhaps because he liked to maintain a sense of proportion about things, at first avoided any dramatic steps. The case of the *Popolo Veneto* was very clear and could be explained by the political immaturity of certain young people who were not averse to the "fame" of having themselves talked about. Hence the Patriarch thought that the situation called for discreet action rather than a public reprimand. The weekly, *Il Popolo Veneto*, however, had to suspend publication and on Christmas Day, in 1955, a collective pastoral letter of the Bishops of the Venetian province clearly denounced the error of the "opening to the Left." But these warnings were not enough and eight months later, on August 16, 1956, the Patriarch had to intervene directly with a pastoral letter that left no room for any misunderstandings.

It is worth while to reproduce a few exerpts from this important document because they reveal the character of Angelo Giuseppe Roncalli and his methods of procedure.

". . . With a particular sense of regret I must stress my awareness of the persistence shown by some in supporting *at any cost* the so-called opening to the Left, in opposition to the clear position of the hierarchy of the Church, made clear in the August verbal and written pronouncements of the Holy Father, and most evident in the Christmas Message of the Tri-Venetian episcopate, and in successive communications repeated publicly and privately in the form of friendly persuasion.

"Even on this point it is painful to me to point out that as Catholics we again find ourselves face to face with a very grave doctrinal error, and before a flagrant violation of Catholic discipline. The error lies in participating, at the level of practice, and sharing the ideology of Marxism, which is the negation of Christianity and whose applications cannot be reconciled with the presuppositions of the Gospel of Christ.

"Either we are with the Church and we follow its directions, and thereby merit the name of Catholics, or we prefer to do things on our own, promoting and fostering divisions and assuming the responsibilities thereof. In such a case the name of Catholic no longer befits us."

Cardinal Roncalli had hoped that his loving and direct summons to return to reason would suffice. But when he realized that these discreet interventions were not enough, he did not hesitate to interfere in a most solemn way to defend the doctrinal moral principles which are sacrosanct for the Church and therefore unchangeable.

This did not prevent the Patriarch from addressing a message to his flock, six months later, exhorting them to welcome the delegates to the Congress of the Italian Socialist Party being held in Venice. To appreciate this gesture it must be pointed out that the Italian Socialist Party—which has nothing in common with other European Socialist parties—is closely linked to Communism.

In this letter the Venetians were exhorted not to belie the fame of their traditional hospitality, but the Patriarch reminded them that "an economic and social system cannot be solidly built on foundations that are not those established by Christ," even though the holding of the socialist congress denoted an effort to arrive at an agreement leading to a betterment of living conditions.

These incidents, contradictory on the surface, led to talk that the Cardinal who was a "rightist" had now veered to the "left." In reality the Patriarch was only the shepherd who watches over his flock to keep them on the path of truth. If any lesson can be drawn from these Venetian episodes it is only that with respect to partisan politics Cardinal Roncalli was of the view that the Church should take an attitude of great reserve.

Church authorities should intervene only when, other attempts at persuasion having failed, there arises a real danger of inadmissable doctrinal or moral concessions which compromise and menace Catholic orthodoxy and the welfare of souls.

After a residence of five years in Venice, the Patriarch left his beloved city on the morning of October 12, 1958, to attend the conclave of Cardinals that would elect a new Pope. He went to the golden basilica to say before the altar of Mark the Evangelist the *Itinerarium Clericorum,* the liturgical prayer for ecclesiastics about to embark on a journey. He prayed before the Blessed Sacrament and the image of the Nicopœia Madonna. Then he imparted a blessing to those who had gathered around him to bid him good-by. As his boat proceeded down the Grand Canal along the entire way from the quay of St. Mark's to the railroad station, the crowds recognized him and waved him an affectionate farewell.

At the station church authorities and a throng of the faithful renewed their farewells to the Patriarch. There was a portent in the air and this portent perhaps was felt by the Cardinal Patriarch himself. As he acknowledged the last greetings from the window of the train, he was smiling and deeply moved. "What can you do? Everybody wishes me well. For me the best wish is that I may be able to return here to Venice in two weeks."

The train moved slowly out of the station. Their Patriarch was leaving never to return. Before parting from his flock in Venice he had expressed his thanks to them for the tribute of sorrow and prayer they had rendered to Pius XII, and to ask them for prayers "so that the modest and very humble contribution that the Cardinal of the titular church of Saint Prisca and the Patriarch of Venice can make in the way of advice and cooperation in the election of the new Pontiff may be a true consolation for the Church and of benefit to souls."

Venice, like Bergamo, was indelibly printed in his heart. Before him stood Rome and the vacant Apostolic See. Soon there would be another Pontiff in the chair of St. Peter. *"Procedamus in pace"* (let us proceed in peace), says the *Itinerarium Clericorum.*

VII

....

"Vocabor Joannes"

AFTER THE DEATH of Pius XII the sorrow of the civilized world was directed toward Rome, merging with the filial mourning and prayers of Catholics. The transport of the bier of the Pope from Castel Gandolfo to the Vatican was a sad triumphal march in which hundreds of thousands of persons paid tribute to the work and memory of Eugenio Pacelli, "*Defensor Civitatis.*" An immense and veritable pilgrimage took place during the three days in which the remains of the deceased Pope lay in state in the center of the Vatican basilica at the very place where Pius XII had been accustomed to stop and address pilgrims during general audiences. It was also the spot where in February 1946 and again in January 1953 there had been raised the throne from which Pope Pius had presented the newly nominated cardinals with their red hats, among them Cardinal Roncalli.

The Patriarch of Venice was present among the members of the Senate of the Church on the day of the final farewell to Eugenio Pacelli. On this day the Pope's body was enclosed in three coffins for preservation through the centuries, and then was slowly lowered into the grottoes to be placed directly before the tomb of the apostle Peter.

Cardinal Roncalli met every morning with his eminent colleagues in the general congregations which assembled under the presidency of the Cardinal Dean, Eugene Tisserant, in order to make preparations for the conclave. With each passing day the august gathering that met in the hall of the Consistory on the second floor of the Apostolic Palace became larger and larger. Cardinals were arriving from every part of the world. The Cardinal Primate of Poland, Stefan Wyszynski, Archbishop of Gniezno and Warsaw, was given an especially warm reception. Would the two other cardinals from behind the Iron Curtain also come?

From his confinement in Krasic, the Archbishop of Zagreb had sent word immediately after the announcement of the Pope's death that he was too ill to go to Rome. Apart from his illness, which was real, Cardinal Stepinac thought that the Belgrade government might authorize his journey to Rome but not his return to Yugoslavia. Although confined in Krasic, his native village, the Cardinal is in his diocesan territory and on occasion he can receive his vicars general. Thus, although he has been prevented from governing his diocese since the day of the unjust sentence that condemned him, morally at least he is still the Archbishop of Zagreb. Hence he did not want to abandon his faithful, even temporarily, if he were not certain of being able to return to them.

The case of Cardinal Mindszenty, Primate of Hungary, was quite different. He had been released from prison when the insurrection of 1956 had seemed successful and was rehabilitated by the government which ruled the country for a few hopeful days. But when the merciless repression began with the second Soviet intervention, he was forced to ask for political asylum from the American Legation in Budapest. The Communist proconsuls, restored to power by Red Army tanks, charged him with co-responsibility in the insurrection despite the fact he had been strictly isolated since the day of his condemnation in 1949. They declared his rehabilitation invalid and stated that the Primate was "guilty of treason" and would be placed under arrest if he left the United States Legation where he has been interned for the past two years.

What would Cardinal Mindszenty do? He, like all the other cardinals, had received the announcement of the Pope's death and an invitation from the Dean of the Sacred College to attend the conclave which would elect a new Pontiff. This was in accordance with Article 39 of the apostolic constitution *Vacantis Apostolicae Sedis* which regulates the election of the Roman Pontiff. "We order all the Cardinals to obey, by virtue of holy obedience, the letter of notification by presenting themselves immediately, if they are not detained by a legitimate hindrance, to the place indicated therein for the election of the Pope as soon as they shall have been informed by the Cardinal Dean, or if he be prevented by another Cardinal, of the vacancy of the Apostolic

Chair and are summoned to elect a new Pontiff. . . ."

The first prerogative of the cardinals of the Roman Catholic Church is that of electing the Pope. Hence it is evident that theirs is not only the right but the duty to participate in the conclave. This consideration was raised in Italian circles and not a few saw in it a kind of order to Cardinal Mindszenty.

In reality, as we have said, the Primate of Hungary received the invitation sent to all the members of the College of Cardinals. The American government then asked the Sacred College whether the U. S. Legation in Budapest should make an effort to facilitate the Primate's journey to Rome, although obviously he would never be able to return to his country. After being so authorized, the American *chargé d'affaires* asked the Budapest government for a pass of safe-conduct for the eminent refugee. In reply, the Communist government not only refused but accused the United States government of interference in Hungary's internal affairs because it was interceding on behalf of a "political delinquent," condemned by a lawful court of his own country. The United States Legation was justifiably concerned that no person who had requested and obtained the right to its asylum be arrested at the door as soon as he left his refuge as had happened earlier to Nagy when he left the Yugoslav embassy in Budapest.

Did the Hungarian government desire the Sacred College to intervene directly on Cardinal Mindszenty's behalf in order to exploit this later for propaganda purposes? This we do not know. The fact remains that the cardinals did not intercede and that the Primate of Hungary did not go to Rome, even though all preparations had been made to welcome him at the conclave.

As Cardinal Roncalli took part every morning in the general congregations, the "enclosure of the conclave" was being feverishly prepared in the Apostolic Palaces. The electors of a Pope must strictly isolate themselves during the election, without any communication with the outside world. Although the Vatican is a complex of buildings, and one of the largest structures in the world, it does not have enough apartments to receive and accommodate the more than fifty princes of the Church with their conclavists (each is accompanied by an ecclesiastical secretary and a servant). It was therefore necessary to provide improvised lodgings by taking over offices, dividing up corridors and reception rooms so as to make "cells" for each cardinal and his companions.

Above all it was necessary to establish an enclosure walled off from the outside world. This was done by building temporary walls and huge doors that could be carefully sealed off, by disconnecting telephone wires, by painting the windows blue and sealing them, and finally by installing the turn-boxes at the end of the Stairs of Pius IX. These turn-boxes, the *ruote*, under the direct surveillance of the marshal of the Conclave—an hereditary title and privilege of the family of Prince Chigi—were the only way of getting supplies to the cardinals in the walled enclosure. A great hustle and bustle of masons, carpenters, and porters from the Apostolic "Floreria" (the Vatican's maintenance department) prevailed as these things were being done and the cells and the necessary furnishings fitted out.

Cardinal Roncalli, as always, retained his calm in this atmosphere of excitement and expectation. He had his lodgings at the Domus Mariae on the Via Aurelia where he had been assigned a small apartment—a bedroom and study very modestly furnished—on the first floor of the building. The Patriarch celebrated Mass every morning in the adjacent chapel dedicated to the Sacred Heart, and at such an early hour that he always had time to attend a second Mass said by his secretary, Mons. Capovilla. Then he would go to the Vatican and come back a little after 12 P.M. and would take his meals in a separate room on the ground floor. Then, after taking a short rest, during those short autumn afternoons he revisited the scenes of his youth: the Church of Santa Maria in Montesanto on the Piazza del Popolo where he had been ordained a priest, the altar near the tomb of St. Peter where he had celebrated his first Mass, and the old headquarters of the Society for the Propagation of the Faith.

On the afternoon of Saturday, October 25, he left his room at the Domus Mariae, after tidying it up himself as usual, and went to the Vatican to enter the conclave. As he left the building he was greeted by Signorina Alda Miceli, the President of the Young Women's Section of Catholic Action, and the entire household of the Domus Mariae (which belongs to the aforementioned organization). "Pray that I return early," said the Cardinal as he gave her his blessing. And his last greeting to those present was *"Arrividerci."*

On the following morning, a little after 11:30 A.M., the first *fumata*, or smoke signal, rose upward from the chimney of the Sistine Chapel; it was but a brief puff and unmistakably white. An editor of the *Osservatore Romano* who was in the office of the Secretariat of State saw the smoke from a distance of several yards and immediately dashed off to the newspaper in order to prepare an "extra." But as he entered the editorial room he heard the radio announcing that the result of the balloting was negative; a black smoke signal had followed the first white one. The same mistake was repeated on Sunday afternoon.

On Monday morning learned discussions were taking place all over Rome, especially among so-called experts, on the nature and the color of the smoke signal. Some brought forth the most erudite arguments to suggest that it was not so much a question of color as of the quantity of the smoke. The old Moroni ecclesiastical dictionary was leafed through and commented upon. For his part, the marshal of the Conclave, Prince Chigi, a former air force officer, introduced into the Conclave smoke-producing materials such as are used for signaling at airports. This compounded the confusion.

How is the *fumata* traditionally produced? At the end of each negative ballot, the last created of the cardinal deacons burns the ballots, to which he adds some moistened straw, in the stove of the Sistine Chapel. The resulting smoke is or should be black. Only when a candidate has been elected are the ballots burned without straw and the smoke is whitish and scanty. The vagueness of the first *fumata* complicated things. The radio reporters, huddled around their microphones on the temporary platforms which had been put up on St. Peter's Square, were at a complete loss. On Tuesday evening the crowds in the square saw smoke pouring out of the stovepipe of the Sistine Chapel at 5:08 P.M. It appeared white to some and dark to others. But what made everybody in the square feel that the big moment had arrived was the brevity of the signal and the scantiness of the smoke. Minutes went by slowly, then the quarter hours, but the hope became a certainty when lamps were lit behind the curtains of the central window facing the loggia, or balcony, from which papal blessings are imparted. Now all doubt vanished and everyone waited eagerly to learn who had been elected Pope and to receive his first blessing.

The great square and the Via della Conciliazione were thronged with ever swelling crowds. Even the stairs and the place before the basilica swarmed with people. The Marshal's loggia was filled with invited guests, as were the terraces of the adjoining buildings and the slopes of the Janiculum Hill. There were people of all ages and every social class, and an amazing number of foreigners armed with binoculars, which they kept continually aimed at the balcony. The crowd was constantly fed by new streams of people seemingly coming from every point of the compass: column after column of seminarians dressed in black, violet, red, white and blue; endless ranks of pilgrims; groups of the faithful; vendors of photographs and pictures of the cardinals gathered in the conclave.

A large area before the basilica had been roped off and

reserved for the members of the households of the cardinals and the pontifical gendarmerie. Temporary platforms for radio, movie and television apparatus and personnel had been erected just beyond this restricted area. Movie and television equipment had also been installed on the left colonnade overlooking the Sistine Chapel.

The Pope had been elected. But who was he? A tense watch began—on the piazza, in the editorial rooms of news agencies and newspapers ready to rush special editions to the streets.

Someone telephoned the *Osservatore Romano* to announce that the newly-elected Pope was Alfredo Cardinal Ottaviani. The call had been made from the Loggia delle Dame above the entrance of the bronze portal leading into Vatican City. The information was worthy of attention because from this vantage point it would not have been impossible to hear, if the voices were loud enough, something being confidentially discussed behind the windows of the conclave enclosure. The news of Cardinal Ottaviani's "election" was sent out by the press agencies but then prudently stopped. Something similar had happened toward the end of the conclave which had elected Pius XI, when some Roman newspapers had rushed out a special edition announcing the election of Cardinal Tacci and the news had spread so fast in the space of the few minutes between the *fumata* and the solemn announcement that the home town of Cardinal Tacci went wild with joy.

This time the crowds had to wait for forty minutes. The *fumata* had risen upward at 5:08 P.M. and at 6:00 P.M. the windows of the balcony above the central entrance of the basilica were opened. Cardinal Canali, senior deacon of the Holy Roman Church—during the time of the conclave there was news that he was seriously ill—appeared to deliver the traditional formula announcing the long-awaited event: the elected Pope was Angelo Giuseppe Cardinal Roncalli, of the titular Church of St. Prisca and Patriarch of Venice. He spoke in a voice broken with emotion:

"I announce to you a great joy: we have a Pope: the most eminent and reverend Lord Cardinal Roncalli, who has chosen the name of John XXIII."

This announcement was answered by a mighty roar of the crowd which was repeated when the newly elected Pope, preceded by crucifers, appeared on the balcony. The endless masses of people received the first benediction *Urbi et Orbi* in deep silence. It was 6:15 P.M., October 28, 1958.

The editor of the *Osservatore Romano* did publish an "extra," containing a large photograph of Cardinal Roncalli and a biographical sketch of the new Pontiff. The "extra" with its front page adorned with a yellow border —in homage to tradition—was on the streets in twenty minutes.

Meanwhile in the Vatican, prelates and journalists had penetrated the enclosure which they had entered from the portal of the Secretariat of State which overlooks the outer balcony. The Cardinal Dean expelled the intruders and excommunicated them all, but that very evening John XXIII granted them absolution. Such incidents take place during almost every papal election. This time, however, thanks to the energy of Cardinal

Tisserant, the conclave area remained closed. It was not officially opened until the following morning, October 29, shortly after 10:00 A.M. The evening of his election the Pope dined with his cardinals at a common table in the Borgia apartments, and spent the night in the vacant apartment of the Cardinal Secretary of State. As is known, this office had not been filled since the death of Cardinal Maglione in 1944.

What had happened at the conclave? On the following days newspapers and magazines published "revelations" purporting to record the vote tallies for each of the twelve ballotings, the names of all the candidates, and the names of the individual voters.

When, on November 6, the Pope granted an audience to journalists and special correspondents who had been sent from all parts of the world to cover the election, with the customary good-nature of Angelo Roncalli, John XXIII put a summary end to these rumors:

". . . Attempts have been made to guess the secrets of the conclave, and naturally there are not even two lines which correspond to the truth. Even if the efforts of journalists in this respect have been considerable, silence perhaps would have been the best policy . . ."

Two or three days before the conclave began a friend of one of the authors visited a very influential cardinal of the Curia. He did not ask him any indiscreet questions, but only for a summary indication of those cardinals who were *papabili*. He felt free to do this because of the confidential information which this same cardinal had given to him in March 1939, a few hours before the beginning of the very brief conclave that elected Pius XII. In reply the cardinal clearly said that no such indication could be given. In his opinion there were candidacies among this or that group of cardinals, but such candidacies had not been openly discussed and they would be formulated in the conclave only after the trends had been indicated by the first balloting. The selection would be made from a list of names made up at that time.

The cardinal did say, however, that the conclave, despite rumors to the contrary, would not be a very brief one. The visitor thought that this might be a diplomatic reply, and he did not insist. Yet the events that transpired showed that the cardinal had expressed a true estimate of the situation with no second thought.

On the day after the election a French cardinal declared: "These are extraordinary days in which once again one feels something of the mystery of the Church. In the beginning each one proposes the name of the candidate who, in good conscience, seems to him to be the one most worthy of election. Then, little by little, personal differences dissolve; conversations, reflection, prayer, bring forth new elements and the final act is really the gesture of a community which, under the influence of the Holy Ghost, gives to the Church its supreme shepherd. Last Saturday an Italian cardinal told me about an old Roman proverb according to which the first day of the conclave is determined by the devil, the second by men, and the third day by God. John XXIII was elected on the third day."

In a letter to his faithful in Paris, sent from Rome on November 1, Cardinal Feltin wrote:

". . . We were fifty, coming from the most distant lands, and necessarily we all had opinions concerning the problems of our time which in part differed from one another. We knew little about each other; personally I had never met most of my colleagues. But very soon, through personal contact and by the action of the Holy Ghost, ardently invoked, and by entrusting our grave responsibilities to Our Lord, we achieved a community of thought and harmonized our perspectives to arrive finally at the election of John XXIII." [1]

Similar expressions have been made verbally by young ecclesiastics who participated in the conclave as secretaries to the cardinals. It is not possible to know more than this about the three days of the election and about the twelve ballotings which took place between the morning of October 26 and the late afternoon of October 28.

As a matter of fact, the constitution *Vacantis Apostolicae Sedis*, promulgated by Pius XII on December 8, 1945, contains regulations which forbid cardinals and whoever else may participate in a conclave to violate "directly or indirectly," the secrecy of the election. Anyone guilty of this would incur an excommunication reserved in a special manner to the Pope personally for absolution unless the one excommunicated were at the point of death (Art. 61). Therefore anything that is reported about the proceedings of a conclave is but the product of fancy or imagination.

[1] *Documentation Catholique*, vol. LV, p. 1489.

What is known, however, is what happened at the conclusion of the conclave because it is determined by very precise ceremony and ritual. As soon as the last balloting was over, Alfredo Cardinal Ottaviani, the junior cardinal deacon, summoned the prefect of pontifical ceremonies, Mons. Enrico Dante, to the Sistine Chapel. He, in turn, summoned the six masters of ceremonies who immediately had lowered the violet canopies over the cardinals' thrones. The only canopy that remained was the one over the throne of the elected Pope.

Following this, the three cardinals who head the three orders of the Sacred College stepped forward: Tisserant for the cardinal bishops; Van Roey, archbishop of Malines, for the cardinal priests; Canali for the cardinal deacons. They approached the little throne of the Patriarch of Venice, and Cardinal Tisserant, as Dean of the Sacred College, asked him the ritual question in Latin:

"Do you accept your canonically performed election as Supreme Pontiff?"

And the elected Cardinal replied: "Hearing your voice, *'tremens factus sum ego, et timeo'* (I am made to tremble and I fear!). What I know of my poverty and smallness suffices for my confusion. But seeing in the votes of my brothers, the most excellent Cardinals of Our Holy Roman Church, the sign of God's will, I accept the election they have made and I bend my head and my back to the chalice of bitterness and to the yoke of the cross. . . ."

"*Quomodo vis vocari?*" "How do you wish to be called?" Cardinal Tisserant asked him.

"*Vocabor Joannes*." "I shall be called John. This name is sweet to Us because it was Our father's; it is dear because it is the name of the humble parish where We were baptized.

"It is the solemn name of innumerable cathedrals spread about the world, and, first amongst them, of the sacrosanct Lateran Basilica, Our cathedral.

"It is the name which in the long series of the Roman Pontiffs has been most used. Indeed, there have been twenty-two unquestionably legitimate supreme Pontiffs named John. Nearly all had a brief pontificate. We have preferred to shield the smallness of Our own name with this magnificent succession of Roman Pontiffs.

"And was not St. Mark the Evangelist, the glory and protector of Our beloved Venice, he whom St. Peter, Prince of the Apostles and first Bishop of the Roman Church, loved as his own son, also called John?

"But We love the name of John, so dear to Us and to all the Church, particularly because it was borne by two men who were most close to Christ the Lord, the divine redeemer of all the world and founder of the Church: John the Baptist, the precursor of Our Lord . . . and the other John, the beloved disciple and evangelist. . . .

"Venerable Brothers, may God in his mercy grant that We . . . may with the help of divine grace have his same sanctity of life and his strength of soul unto the shedding of our blood, if God so wills."

The three cardinals then retired. Then Mons. Dante, prefect of ceremonies, summoned the Cardinal Deacons Canali and Ottaviani, who followed the newly elected

Pontiff to the sacristy of the Sistine Chapel where the Pope was to receive the white cassock worn by the visible head of the Catholic Church.

The sacristy of the Sistine Chapel is known as the "room of tears." It has indeed been witness to the anxieties that have assailed many Roman Pontiffs after their election as they suddenly became aware of the very grave responsibilities which Providence had entrusted to them. But John XXIII apparently was very calm. He was seized by a burning thirst and he asked for a glass of water. Water was found but there was no glass, so a liturgical chalice was used.

Then he was dressed in the papal robes: white cassock and stockings, red shoes bearing the design of the cross, a white rochet (a linen and lace vestment resembling a surplice), mozzetta, red stole and white zucchetto. Before a conclave, the pontifical tailors prepare the papal robes in three different sizes. This had been done, but this time none of the robes held in readiness were large enough, and the Pope could not button his robe across his chest. His cape of red silk hung well before it but John XXIII, as some perhaps may have noticed, was not able to move his arms freely. (The following night the tailors worked without let-up, and on the morning of October 29 the Pope had robes made to his proper measure. "I felt I was in wraps," he confided to one of his entourage.)

After being dressed for the first time in the papal robes, John XXIII returned to the Sistine Chapel where he blessed the cardinals. Then the new Pontiff mounted the *sedia gestatoria* which was brought to the steps of the altar, and here he received the first homage of the members of the Sacred College: they kissed his hand and were in turn embraced by him. After completing his obedience, Cardinal Tisserant placed the Fisherman's Ring on the finger of the Pope.

After the cardinals, other prelates stepped forward to make their obedience. When it was the turn of Mons. Alberto di Jorio, secretary of the conclave, to kneel before the Pope, John XXIII placed his cardinal's *zucchetto* on the prelate's head in order to signify that from that moment onward he was marked for the purple robes of the cardinalate.

Then the cortege was formed and John XXIII, seated in his *sedia gestatoria* and accompanied by all his cardinals, arrived at the great balcony of St. Peter's basilica, and from there imparted his first benediction, *Urbi et Orbi*. Following this he returned to the Sistine Chapel again to receive the cardinals' homage, as prescribed by rule.

This ceremony was repeated for the third time on the following morning. When it came the turn of the Chinese Cardinal Thomas Tienchensin, who was infirm and seated in a wheelchair, the Pope came down from his throne to receive his homage and embraced him effusively.

At the end of the third obedience the Pope delivered his first public message which voiced many of the deepest concerns of the Papacy in our time. After greeting the bishops, the priests and Catholics all over the world, the Pope's thoughts turned to the persecuted everywhere:

"In a special way Our thoughts go to the bishops, priests, Sisters and all the faithful, who dwell in those nations where the Catholic religion is given none of the freedom due to it or only partial freedom, where men dare to trample on the sacred rights of the Church and where her lawful pastors are expelled or held in custody or so impeded that they cannot discharge their functions properly.

"We wish all to know that We share their sorrows, hardships and distress and that We beg God, the giver of all good things, that someday He may put an end to such inhuman persecutions, which not only hurt the true peace and prosperity of these peoples, but which are also entirely contrary to the civilization of our times and to long acquired human rights.

"May He enlighten the minds of the rulers of these nations with His divine light. May He grant pardon to persecutors. May all enjoy lawful freedom most speedily and may He bestow on them better and happier times.

"With fervent fatherly love We embrace the Universal Church, the Eastern and the Western alike. And to all who are separated from this Apostolic See, where Peter lives in his successors, 'even unto the consummation of the world' (Matt. 28, 20), fulfilling the command of Jesus Christ to bind and loose upon earth (cf. Matt. 16, 19), and to feed the Lord's entire flock, to these We say We open Our heart most lovingly and extend Our open arms.

"Ardently desiring their return to the house of the common Father, We earnestly repeat these words of the divine Redeemer: 'Holy Father, keep in Thy name those whom Thou hast given me that they may be one even as we are' (John 17, 11). For thus 'there shall be one fold and one shepherd' (John 10, 16). We pray, therefore, that all may come willingly and gladly; and by inspiration and the aid of divine grace may it happen as soon as possible.

"No strange house will they find, but their own which indeed was illumined in the past by the eminent doctrine of their forefathers and adorned by their virtue.

"May we be allowed on this occasion to appeal to the rulers of all the nations in whose lands the lot, fortunes and hopes of the various peoples are placed. Why are divisions and disagreements not settled on a fair basis at last? Why are the powers of human ingenuity and natural resources turned so often to the production of arms—destructive instruments of death and ruin—but not to increase the prosperity of all classes of citizens, especially those who live in great poverty.

"We know indeed that huge and complex difficulties stand in the way of accomplishing this praiseworthy purpose and settling the disagreements. These difficulties, however, must be grappled with and overcome, for a most serious project is at issue, one linked most closely with the happiness of the whole human race.

"Take action, then, boldly and with confidence and may heavenly light be given to each of you and may divine aid be yours. Look at the people entrusted to you and listen to their voices. What do they seek, what do they implore from you? Not these new monstrous instruments of war which our times have produced and which can be the cause of fraternal slaughter and annihi-

lation of all—not these, but peace, we say, peace by
which the whole human family may live freely, thrive
and flourish. And justice they seek, by which classes
of society may adjust their mutual rights and duties according to fair standards.

"And finally they seek calm harmony, which alone
can give rise to prosperity worthy of the name. For it is
in peace based on the lawful rights of each person and
sustained by brotherly charity that the highest arts flourish, human talents unite for worthy ends and public and
private resources are increased. You know what men of
lofty minds have thought about this subject. Peace is
'orderly harmony of men' (Augustine, *City of God*,
I, 29, ch. 13). 'Peace is the tranquillity of order' (*ibid.*
and St. Thomas, II–2, 20 Art. 1) and 'the name of peace
is sweet and peace itself is beneficial; but there is a very
great difference between peace and slavery. Peace is
tranquil liberty' (Cicero, *Philip.* 2, 44)."

The speech, in Latin, had been prepared by the Pope
during the night with the collaboration of the secretary
for Latin Letters, Mons. Bacci, and by the substitute
Secretary of State, Mons. Angelo Dell' Acqua.

It might seem that days of such intense activity and
excitement would have shaken any man. But John
XXIII lived through them serenely and calmly. Trusting
in God, he abandoned himself to Him with the simplicity of a child, but with a full consciousness of his
grave responsibilities. He was helped during these moments by the thought of his dead loved ones, ever living and present for him. In his act of acceptance he had

recalled his father, Bishop Radini-Tedeschi, and the prayers of his faithful in Venice, many of whom were already speeding to Rome for his coronation. In an age shaken by political, social and ideological tempests he looked serenely into the future from the height of the chair of St. Peter.

He rose very early on the morning of October 29. Someone during that early hour asked him how he had slept and he answered, "As usual,"—in short, like one who in the fulfilment of duty has found the comfort and assurance necessary to fulfill other duties that will return on the morrow after the pause and rest of the night. He began his day trusting in God, and under the patronage of the Virgin Mary to whom he had been devoted since the first years of his life, and with the help of his protecting saints, especially of St. Charles Borromeo.

It has been noted in these pages that more than one person, including some in extraordinary authority, had predicted that Angelo Roncalli would one day mount the throne of Peter. There is no way of vouching for the authenticity of such reports, but no one has noted the following strange coincidence:

Reproduced in the apostolic constitution regulating the proceedings of a conclave is a sample of the ballot form which gives a name so that the cardinals may fully understand the voting procedure. It is very simple. A single line reads: *"Eligo in Summum Pontificem Rev. mum"* (I elect the most Reverend . . . as Supreme Pontiff). Below there is a line for folding the ballot, and below this line the name of the person chosen is to be written. Now in the facsimile of the apostolic constitution the name used is the following:

"Dominum D. Card. Baronium" (the Lord Cardinal Baronius).

The Oratorian, Cardinal Cesare Baronius, a disciple of St. Philip Neri, had been dead for four centuries, so his name was given merely as an example. But his motto was *"Obedientia et Pax"* (Obedience and Peace), words dear to him and which he would pronounce every day in the Vatican Basilica, resting his head on the foot of the bronze statue of St. Peter, so worn by the kisses of the faithful.

"Obedientia et Pax" were also the words on the coat-of-arms of Angelo Cardinal Roncalli.

VIII

••••••••••••••

"The Promise of a Glorious Reign"

THE WORLD was notified that John XXIII would be crowned on Tuesday, November 4, 1958, through the official *intimatio*, or notice, sent out by the Papal Prefect of Ceremonies. It had been thought that the event would take place at a later date, but now an end was put to speculation.

Why the Holy Father chose this date is not known with certainty. But great tasks awaited him, and it is probable that he did not want the cardinals who headed episcopal sees to remain away from their dioceses longer than was necessary. Another consideration was that November 4th is the feast day of Charles Borromeo, the patron of bishops and a saint for whom Angelo Roncalli, as we have seen, had long had strong devotion.

The coronation of a Pope adds nothing to his papal authority or his jurisdiction—the Pope assumes office from the moment he says, "I accept" to the Dean of the

College of Cardinals immediately after his election. The plenitude of Peter's powers passes to him at that moment.

Nevertheless the age-old coronation ceremonies are not a meaningless pageant. They mark the official beginning of a Pope's reign with the pomp and circumstances befitting his office.

The morning hours of November 4th were overcast and the skies were drizzly. The weather did not prevent thousands and thousands of Romans and 400,000 pilgrims from crowding into the great Square of St. Peter. Forty thousand of the more fortunate who had received invitations and tickets were able to enter the interior of the basilica. Among them were diplomats and representatives of heads of governments, of religious orders, and of Catholic organizations throughout the world.

Tu es Petrus (Thou art Peter) sang the choir as the procession accompanying the 262nd supreme Pontiff of the Catholic Church, borne upon his *sedia gestatoria*, filed into St. Peter's. Three times during the progress to the main altar one of the six masters of ceremonies lighted a small brazier of glowing coals and handed a handful of flax to the Pope. As he threw it upon the flame it burned brightly for a moment and then went out, leaving a disagreeable odor. Each time the master of ceremonies sang: "*Pater sancte, sic transit gloria mundi*" (Holy Father, so passes the glory of the world), in order to recall to the Head of the Universal Church at the very moment of his elevation that human honor is nothing before God and that the material world will crumble and vanish.

(Centuries ago together with the burning flax the Pope was also presented with the bronze figure of a cock to remind him of Peter's thrice-repeated denial on the night of Gethsemane—today the bronze cock is merely an ornament in the sacristy of the basilica.)

The long ceremonial of the Mass reached its climax when the pallium, a circular band of white wool symbolizing the fullness of episcopal power, was placed upon the Pope and when he received the obedience of the cardinals, patriarchs, bishops and other prelates who passed before his throne. The Mass ended and the Pope was borne to the huge balcony of St. Peter's that faces the Square.

It was 12:50 P.M. when Cardinal Canali, Dean of the Cardinal Deacons, placed the crown on the head of John XXIII with these words: "Receive the tiara adorned with three crowns and know that you are the Father of princes and kings, Pontiff of the whole world, and Vicar on earth of Our Lord Jesus Christ to whom be honor and glory for ever and ever."

The three crowns of the papal tiara signify the sanctifying, teaching and governing powers of the Church; there are various other interpretations of its meaning. All the ceremonies of the Mass and coronation are deeply symbolic and are prescribed by ancient custom.

In one respect Pope John departed from the usual ceremonial of the coronation when he delivered a homily during the Mass. A papal homily, by long-established usage, is a familiar and intimate talk given by a Pope to a bishop and his immediate flock. But now, due to modern means of communication, the new Pope could reach out and embrace in an equally intimate way his entire flock throughout the world, and he seized this opportunity.

"We have at heart in a very special manner Our task as Shepherd of the entire flock." With these words, John XXIII announced the mission of his pontificate. He would take no notice, other than to deny them, of various labels placed upon his reign. He did not intend to be a diplomat, a scientist, or a sociologist. The duties of these could be considered as a complement to a Pope's work and were, to be sure, important. Yet it was more important to gather around himself the ranks of all Christians; to teach them the ways of salvation; to guide them by word and by example toward the goal of perfection; to defend them against the threats of their enemies.

Even before his election Angelo Cardinal Roncalli had a well-defined concept of those things which were needed from the new Pope. This is shown in a revealing document, a letter he wrote to Bishop Piazzi of Bergamo shortly before he entered the conclave. After a plea for the prayers of the Bishop and his faithful it reads:

". . . As I am about to enter the Conclave . . . my soul is comforted with the hope that the new Pentecost may bestow upon the Church, through the renewal of its Head and the reconstitution of its ecclesiastical structure, a new vigor in bringing about the victory of truth and peace. Our mutual prayers must obtain for us that he be a man of wise and mild rule, that he be a saint and a sanctifier of souls. You understand me, Excellency. I greet and embrace you. And again a blessing upon your faithful."

The three aspects of this program—the victory of truth, goodness and peace, a wise and mild rule, and the sanctification of souls—were inseparable from the reconstitution of the Church's organization, weakened by many deaths and vacancies. At the very moment of his election John XXIII had clearly demonstrated his intention of putting his program into practice without any delay. The designation as a cardinal of Mons. Alberto di Jorio, secretary of the conclave, took place, as has been mentioned, in the Sistine Chapel on the evening of October 28th. The Pope thus revived a custom of the Roman Curia according to which the secretary of the conclave is elevated to the purple.

On October 29 came the announcement that Mons. Federico Callori di Vignale had been nominated as Majordomo of His Holiness. This post had been vacant for many years. At the same time the only surviving participating private chamberlain, Mons. Mario Nasalli Rocca di Corneliano, was promoted to the post of Maestro di Camera, and four new participating private chamberlains were named. Thus the "noble ante-chamber" was restored to its full efficiency.

The faithful Mons. Loris Capovilla, who followed Cardinal Roncalli to Rome from Venice, refused an honorary post and was content to remain simply as the Pope's personal secretary. It seems that he had expressed a desire to return to Venice, something which the household chauffeur, Guido Gusso, also wanted to do. Informed of their intentions, John XXIII is supposed to have said: "Well then, I'll go back to Venice too!"

These first nominations, naturally, were restricted to the pontifical court. However, they demonstrated that the Pope "abhors a vacuum," and that he does not like to have posts empty in the papal household or in the Curia.

On that same day an important nomination was made in order to fill one of the most serious vacancies in the Roman Curia. On October 29th, around 1:00 P.M., an editor of the *Osservatore Romano* was called into the Secretariat of State and was handed the following bulletin with instructions to keep it secret until 2:00 P.M.:

"His Holiness has deigned to name His Excellency Mons. Domenico Tardini as his Pro-Secretary of State."

The Pope's action in appointing as Pro-Secretary of State a prelate not yet a cardinal was not without precedent. When the Patriarch of Venice, Giuseppe Sarto, was elected to the throne of Peter on August 4, 1903, and assumed the name of Pius X, he called to his side Bishop Rafael Merry del Val to serve as Pro-Secretary of State. Another Patriarch of Venice, now John XXIII, chose for the same office Monsignor Domenico Tardini.

The post of Secretary of State had been vacant since the death of Luigi Cardinal Maglione in his native town of Casoria on August 22, 1944. Since that time the functions of this high office had been carried out personally by Pius XII with the collaboration of the Secretary of the Congregation of Extraordinary Affairs, Mons. Domenico Tardini, head of the first section of the

Pope Pius XII and Cardinal Roncalli

Cardinal Roncalli casts vote in Italian election of May 5, 1958

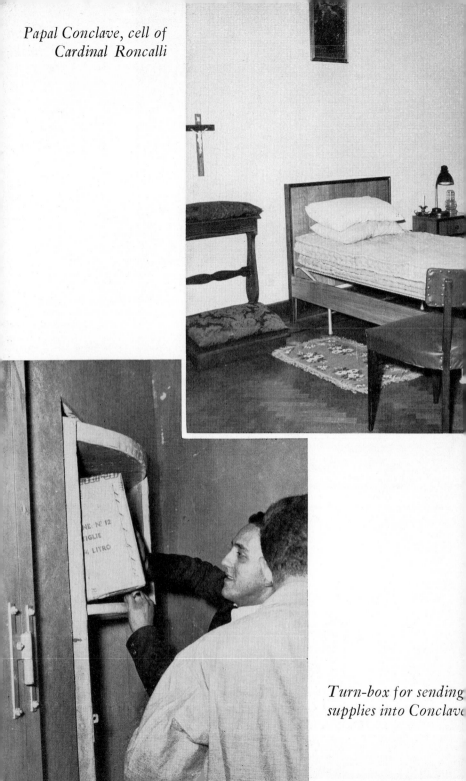

Papal Conclave, cell of
Cardinal Roncalli

Turn-box for sending
supplies into Conclave

John XXIII receiving obedience of Cardinals immediately after election

Cardinal Ruffini and Cardinal Spellman offer their homage

*First blessing to the City and the World
from balcony of St. Peter's*

At Mass of Coronation

Cardinal Tardini
Papal Secretary of State

At College of the Propaganda Fide

Pope John XXIII in his study

*Coat-of-arms of
Pope John XXIII*

Secretariat of State (Extraordinary Affairs), and by Mons. Gian Battista Montini, Substitute of the second section of the same department (Ordinary Affairs).

At the time of the second consistory of his pontificate —in January 1953—Pius XII had wished to appoint his two most valuable and devoted collaborators to the Sacred College. But they begged the Holy Father to leave them as they were. In his allocution to the cardinals the Pope spoke of this unusual renunciation and warmly eulogized the two monsignori who received the titles of Pro-Secretaries of State for their respective sections. This, in fact, meant that the real Secretary of State was the Pope.

Later Monsignor Montini was appointed archbishop of Milan and his duties were assumed by the Substitute, Mons. Angelo Dell'Acqua.

Mons. Tardini is a man of sturdy, medium-sized build. A thick crop of gray hair, cut short, covers his head and the expressive eyes behind his glasses are at once inquiring, humorous, and ironic. His gait, slow but sure, reminds one of an old sailor.

His character is marked by a deep attachment to truth which he proclaims frankly and in disregard of consequences, although he often couches his words in jocular language. His limitless charity is applied with gruff and masculine gentleness. He serves justice with ability and intelligence and although he is devoted in his friendships he does not allow them to influence his judgments.

Mons. Tardini was born in Rome on February 29,

1888. Having completed his studies at the old Pontifical Seminary of St. Apollinare—where he was a student at the same time as Angelo Roncalli—he received the degrees of doctor of philosophy and doctor of theology and was ordained September 20, 1912.

For some years he taught sacramental theology and liturgy in the new Pontifical Seminary of the Lateran and at the Pontifical University of the Progaganda Fide. During this time he published (in 1923) a textbook on sacramental theology noted for its clarity and doctrinal exactness.

In 1920 he was appointed a consultor of the Congregation of the Sacraments and, in 1921, a *minutante* of the Congregation of Extraordinary Ecclesiastical Affairs. It was also during this period that he acted as ecclesiastical director of the national men's Catholic Action organization and of the Italian Catholic youth organization. In 1929 he was promoted to the position of Undersecretary of the Congregation of Extraordinary Ecclesiastical Affairs. In 1933 he became a member of the Pontifical Commission "Pro Russia."

It was Pius XI who, in 1935, named him Substitute in the Papal Secretariat of State and also Secretary of the Code, and the following year a consultor of the Supreme Congregation of the Holy Office. In 1937 he became Secretary of the Congregation of Extraordinary Ecclesiastical Affairs to succeed Mons. Giuseppe Pizzardo who was created a cardinal. Mons. Tardini has also served as a consultor of the Congregation of the Consistory, as President of the Commission "Pro Russia," and, since

1944, as a consultor of the Congregation for the Oriental Church.

Much could be written concerning the abilities and good-natured character of Mons. Domenico Tardini but it is his deep charity which attracts us. This is displayed in his devotion to Villa Nazareth, the school for boys of above-average intelligence which he founded in Rome with the aid of American friends and in which he spends all his spare time, gives his personal attention to the up-bringing of each child, concerns himself with the pro-gram of studies, and plays with the boys at recreation.

The origins of this institution go back to 1944 when he read in a newspaper that a small orphanage, con-ducted by an elderly and pious lady, had been bombed and was being moved to a new location at the foot of the Pincian Hill on the Piazza del Popolo. Mons. Tardini then told a trusted friend that for a long time he had wanted to interest himself in a work for orphans al-though he had not decided whether to found a new home or to assist one already established.

"See this," he said, holding up the newspaper. "Go, find out what you can about conditions there and let me know what can be done."

The messenger visited the orphanage in its new quar-ters and discovered it was in grave difficulties. "Let us go to see it together," Mons. Tardini told him, "but be careful not to call me 'Excellency.' I am merely Don Domenico."

When he and his confidant visited the little school he discovered that its difficulties were not only material

—which was remediable—but that the directress, an Augustinian tertiary, although certainly zealous and kindly, lacked a comprehension of the methods of modern pedagogy. Don Domenico did not believe the little school held the possibilities he was seeking and gave up the idea of adopting it. Nevertheless he did not abandon the orphanage: generous but anonymous gifts of food were made to it continually.

Don Domenico was certain that something new must be attempted.

"There are so many schools for deficient children," he said, "but what about the 'efficient' ones—those who are gifted with an above-average intelligence?" He wanted to help poor children, belonging to large families or orphaned, who showed unusual intelligence and high moral qualities and who could be trained to become leaders in various walks of life.

Some time after his visit to the orphanage on the Pincian Hill he asked his friend to look for a suitable building in the suburbs of Rome. The word was passed to other friends and acquaintances and eventually it became known that a house, surrounded by a beautiful garden and located near a small pine wood, was up for sale.

Mons. Tardini went to see it; he was pleased both with the house and its surroundings. Thus Villa Nazareth came into being. Today, greatly enlarged and improved and even more beautiful, it is under the direction of the Sisters of Charity of Cincinnati (Ohio), a congregation that has contributed so much to education and hospital care. The flourishing institution is the pride and joy of

Mons. Tardini and the most tangible monument to his charity, for there are many other kindly deeds of which we shall never know.

Mons. Tardini's post as Pro-Secretary of State lasted for only a few weeks. On November 17th the Pope received in audience all the members of the Secretariat of State headed by Mons. Tardini, who presented the homage of the staff to Pope John XXIII. The Holy Father answered slowly, in the almost conversational tone which he used during the first days of his pontificate. He began by declaring that he did not wish to linger over prefixes and suffixes. In order to start things off he was going to abolish one of them then and there: from that moment onward Mons. Tardini was no longer Pro-Secretary but Secretary of State of the Pope.

For those versed in the ways of the Vatican this declaration could but be the prelude to another long-awaited papal announcement: the calling of a consistory for the appointment of new cardinals. The ranks of the Sacred College were severely depleted. Since the time of Sixtus V (1586) its membership had been fixed at seventy, but when Pope John was elected there were only fifty-two members, and more than twelve of these were over eighty years of age.

It had been clear ever since the day of his election that the Pope intended to proceed with the nomination of new cardinals immediately. This intention was emphasized by the incident with Mons. Di Jorio. In addition, the Pope had extended a cordial greeting to Cardinal Gaetano Cicognani when the Prefect of the Sacred Congregation of Rites had kneeled to make his obedience in the Sistine Chapel. "Write to your brother," John XXIII told him, "that we shall soon have some good news for him." The brother of Cardinal Cicognani was, of course, Archbishop Amleto Cicognani, who had been since 1933 the Apostolic Delegate in Washington.

At 1:00 P.M. on November 17, 1958, it was officially announced that the first consistory of Pope John's pontificate would be held on December 15, 1958. This development was expected, but the news that the new Pope would increase the number of cardinals from seventy to seventy-five, breaking a tradition of nearly four centuries, caused more of a sensation.

As has been said, the apostolic constitution *Postquam*, promulgated by Pope Sixtus V, fixed the number of cardinals at seventy (six from the order of bishops, fifty from the order of priests, fourteen from the order of deacons). John XXIII now named twenty-three new cardinals, thereby exceeding the full complement of Sixtus V by five. So complex and widespread had the Church's affairs become that Pius XII had already been planning to do this, as he indicated in his 1945 Christmas message when announcing his first consistory. But he had then given up the idea in order not to break the custom, even though he realized that the successors of Sixtus V were not bound by his provisions, and that the Pope could raise the limit to any number that he saw fit.

Thus without the necessity of promulgating any law John XXIII increased the number of cardinals. In his view, perhaps, this figure does not yet represent the full complement. It is possible that the present figure was chosen because the number of suburbicarian sees, of cardinalate titles and deaconries are exactly seventy-five. In order to further new appointments the Pope would have to establish new titles and other deaconries. It well may be that he is giving this matter some thought.

Meanwhile as a result of this first consistory, John XXIII has filled the vacancies in the Sacred College and above all, has brought eleven more cardinals into the Roman Curia. These cardinals are the Pope's closest advisers and collaborators in the central administration of the Church.

Disappointment has been expressed in some countries over failure to raise certain archbishops to the cardinalate. Holland had expected that the red hat would be bestowed on the Archbishop of Utrecht, while in the Philippines it was hoped that the Archbishop of Manila would be elevated to the purple. It has been pointed out in some quarters that the Pope has so far failed to name new cardinals in Asia or Africa where the Church is faced both with grave problems and great opportunities. But what was not done in December 1958 may well come to pass at any time.

Moreover the new Pope has already shown evidence of skill and vigor in diplomacy by giving Latin America, where the condition of the Church is critical because of the shortage of clergy, its first cardinals in Uruguay and Mexico. Another evidence is the elevation in rank of the vigorous young Bishop Julius Doepfner of embattled Berlin. At forty-five, Doepfner is by eight years the youngest member of the College of Cardinals.

The twenty-three cardinals created by John XXIII come from twelve countries. Of these two are Americans: Archbishop Cushing of Boston and Archbishop O'Hara of Philadelphia. It is quite possible that in the next consistory the Pope will create still another American cardinal, giving to the United States a total of five. Which American archdiocese will be so honored is, of course, not known; nevertheless it is highly probable that Chicago, which gave to the United States a Mundelein and a Stritch, is at the forefront for consideration. It can be too, that the Holy Father, remembering the historic role of Baltimore, its John Carroll and James Gibbons, will choose another prince of the Church for this venerable archdiocese.

The high regard and affection in which John XXIII holds the Catholics of the United States, and indeed all Americans, was expressed by him in a special audience in which after the bestowal of the red hat on all the newly-elevated in the consistory of December 15, 1958, he received the cardinals of the United States headed by Cardinal Spellman and accompanied by other American ecclesiastical and lay dignitaries.

Another appointment attests Angelo Roncalli's desire to make known his veneration for the memory of Pius XI. One of the first nominations to the cardinalate included Mons. Carlo Confalonieri, former Archbishop of Aquila, at present Secretary of the Holy Congregation of Seminaries and Universities. The elevation of this prelate occasioned some surprise in Curial circles, but aside from the fact of seniority in the Curia it must be recalled that Mons. Confalonieri, together with another Lombard priest, Mons. Diego Venini (now Secret Almoner of His Holiness), was very close to Pius XI as his Participating Private Chamberlain.

Mons. Confalonieri was the author of a biography of Achille Ratti which had greatly pleased Cardinal Roncalli because of its sympathetic portrayal of the character of Pius XI. Confalonieri had been summoned to Rome as a young priest by this Pope and had met on the train a kindly and benevolent ecclesiastic who gave him his first briefing in the ways of the Curia. After their arrival in Rome the prelate had shown him the way to the hospice for priests on the Via del Mascherone. This friendly ecclesiastic was none other than Angelo Roncalli. Pope John recalled this incident but recently to the newly-created Cardinal Confalonieri.

It should be noted that at the consistory the list of new cardinals was headed by the name of the Archbishop of Milan, Gian Battista Montini. Thus he is the *"prima creatura"* of John XXIII and the first in the order of precedence in the Sacred College. This papal gesture reflects the esteem of the new Pope, and there are still other reasons for the consideration accorded to the Archbishop of Milan. In 1953 when Monsignors Montini and Tardini declined the red hat, Pope Pius XII nonetheless wished to confer on them all the privileges of a cardinal. To this he added another honor: after the cardinals they should be accorded precedence over all other ecclesiastical dignitaries.

When the list was drawn up at the time of the consistory, Mons. Tardini insisted that he be appointed a cardinal in the lower order of deacons, thus leaving precedence to his former colleague and friend in the Secretariat of State, Mons. Montini who was to become a cardinal priest.[1] There has been talk in recent years of the rivalry between these prelates. Mons. Tardini's gesture publicly belies these rumors and he has often been heard to declare that "we love one another like brothers."

After moving swiftly to restore the governing body of the Church to its full powers and to give it prestige on formal occasions, the Pope has carried on the pressing duties of the Papacy with great dispatch. He immediately restored the practice of giving regular audiences to the Curia cardinals, a custom that had been discontinued for four years. During the stay of non-Italian cardinals in Rome he took advantage of their presence to discuss with them in detail the conditions in their countries. He has learned his way around the papal domain of Vatican City and has worked his way through a massive accumulation of office work and ritual.

His visits in Rome to the Gesù Bambino hospital for children and to the communal hospital of the Holy Ghost on Christmas Day showed his concern for the humblest of his children. But most memorable of all was his visit to the huge Regina Coeli prison on the 26th of December about which so much has been reported. This

[1] In the secret consistory held December 15, 1958, the Pope appointed Cardinal Tardini as titular archbishop of Laodicea in Syria and he was consecrated by Pope John XXIII in St. Peter's Basilica on December 27, 1958. In this manner Cardinal Tardini later entered the order of cardinal priests and was given the titular Church of Saint Apollinaris. Cardinal Tardini accepted the episcopal dignity because it is the Cardinal Secretary of State who customarily is the consecrator of new papal nuncios and apostolic delegates, but this does not affect the status of Cardinal Montini.

was the first visit a Pope had made to a jail since before 1870. The announcement of the visit caught city officials by surprise, and it is told that the superintendent of the Regina Coeli upon hearing the news, shouted "Who?" On being assured that it was indeed Pope John who was expected, he remarked that bishops require no special pass to enter a prison, and that "the Bishop of Rome, of course, can come any time."

To the chair of St. Peter John XXIII has brought the personal traits that were always characteristic of Angelo Giuseppe Roncalli. He likes to move around, go out and talk with people. In the first month of his pontificate, in addition to visiting St. John Lateran, the cathedral of the Bishop of Rome of which each new pontiff must take formal possession, he has visited the papal summer residence in Castel Gandolfo, the Pontifical Major Roman Seminary, the Lateran Athenaeum, and the Urban College under the auspices of the Propaganda Fide on the Janiculum Hill. On December 8th he went to the Church of Santa Maria Maggiore to celebrate the feast of the Immaculate Conception, and paid a visit of homage to the statue of the Virgin overlooking the Piazza di Spagna.

On January 21, 1959, the police were dismayed when, without notifying them of his intention, he appeared on a visit to a home for retired and infirm priests accompanied only by two members of his household.

The Vatican already hums with anecdotes about John XXIII. Pius XII never took time away from his work, not even for an instant. Even during the hour he walked each day in the gardens he continued to study and did not like to be disturbed.

John XXIII is of a different stamp and the possibility of meeting the Pope has created a new atmosphere, long forgotten, among the personnel of the Vatican.

The Governor-Regent of the State of Vatican City asked the Pope if he should close the entrance to the cupola of St. Peter's during the hour that he takes his walk.

"Why?"

"Because the people might be able to look down and see Your Holiness."

"Oh, we'll conduct ourselves properly and give rise to no scandal," was Pope John's rejoinder.

He took his first walk in the gardens on the afternoon of October 30th. Since it is his custom to have a fixed destination, he went to the buildings of the radio station built high in the old tower of Leo IV. As he arrived, the employees of the radio station were just leaving their work at the end of the day. On seeing the Pope the police on duty tried to make the employees return to the building. John XXIII stopped them and said,

"But why? I'm not exactly the devil."

Then he began to talk with the radio operators, asking each of them questions about his home and family, and with a kindly word for everyone. On the following days he again visited the radio station and talked to the employees.

Another day he asked that he be met at the Lourdes Shrine in the Vatican garden by the superiors and students of the Pontifical Ethiopian College—the only seminary in Vatican City—and he spent some thirty minutes with them in affable conversation.

Workers in Vatican City tell of having met the Pope and kissed his ring and of having been engaged in cordial conversations. In shops, garages, and warehouses all the workers look forward to his sudden appearance in the afternoon hours.

In his audiences "Papa Giovanni," as he is called in Rome, does not belie the reputation of Cardinal Roncalli. Monsignor Josef Hoefer, advisory consultor of the German Embassy to Vatican City, was received by the Pope toward the end of November. He told His Holiness that he had once presented Pius XII with the first two volumes of a theological dictionary of which he was the editor, and then added:

"They are bound volumes and bear the coat-of-arms of Pius XII. But may I be permitted to present the same two volumes with the coat-of-arms of Your Holiness?"

"Look, Monsignor," replied John XXIII, "a kind of socialism reigns here. The volumes you gave to my predecessor are perfectly all right for me. If you wish you may put my coat-of-arms on the third volume when it comes out."

Thus does Pope John XXIII draw to himself affectionate sympathy, and love and devotion for the person of the Pope from all who surround him.

Conclusion

"Father and Shepherd"

IN HIS LAST SPEECH made in Paris, on January 1, 1953, Nuncio Roncalli quoted La Fontaine:

> *"Troublez l'eau, vous y voyez-vous?*
> *Laissez-la reposer.*
> *Vous verrez alors votre image . . ."*
> (Disturb the water, do you see yourself therein?
> Let it settle.
> You will then see yourself.)

Then he added: "May God grant that this teaching, epitomized in the 'Know Thyself' engraved over the entrance of the Delphi Temple, be understood beyond its application to the life of the individual and be even more generously applied whenever there is responsibility to be exercised in the service of the common welfare."

Thus in speaking for the last time before the President of the French Republic as dean of the diplomatic corps, Mons. Roncalli recalled the injunction "Know Thyself." It was the motto by which he lived, and by which he had always encouraged others to live. This he had made clear when as a young priest he had this inscription placed under the huge mirror in the student home he founded in Bergamo.

After his election a French periodical [1] published a penetrating biographical sketch of Pope John XXIII, written after a study of many documents and interviews with those who knew him. It ended: "The picture that we have traced in no wise differs from that which Cardinal Roncalli himself traced for the members of his own diocese."

The periodical was referring, of course, to the first speech of the Patriarch delivered to his faithful in Venice in the basilica of St. Mark. At the beginning of each phase of his career Angelo Giuseppe Roncalli has always presented himself in a spirit of humility, but with self-assurance. We have seen him do this also in Paris in 1945 at the start of his difficult mission, and in the Sistine Chapel immediately following his election.

The words of the ancient sage, "Know Thyself," had been a guide to him from his earliest youth. He has enriched them, made them ever more intimate, filled them with Christian significance.

For petty souls such a discipline is not without its dangers. There is the risk of withdrawal from others and of spiritual aridity. There is also to be avoided a form of sterile self-contemplation, and finally another danger— which is the most serious—of considering oneself perfect and of confusing one's own will with that of Divine Providence. This is a disease from which Angelo Giuseppe Roncalli does not suffer.

[1] *Informations catholiques internationales,* Paris, Nov. 15, 1958.

The Pope has always examined his own thoughts and actions attentively. Perhaps his habit of setting down notes in a diary at the end of each day originated in his continuous exercise of self-scrutiny. The fact that he is keeping this diary is no secret because he himself willingly mentions it to his intimates, to whom he has sometimes said: "Would you like to know what I have written and what I have said about you? Well, I shan't tell you!"

The gifts of a great heart, of absolute sincerity, of rocklike faith and boundless charity lead him to see himself reflected in his fellowmen. In seeking himself he has also found his fellows. Aware of his own limitations —a sign of true intelligence—he knows and respects those of others. To love others as oneself is for him the fundamental law of the Gospel.

This is the man. And to the Chair of Peter he brings all his humanity. In every phase of his life he has been responsive to his duties: as seminarian, priest, bishop, diplomat. But before all else he has been responsible to God and to his own conscience.

These are some of his personal characteristics as described by Monsignor Loris Capovilla, personal secretary of His Holiness.

"He never took aimless walks either in Paris or Venice. But he would go out very gladly whenever it was necessary to visit churches, institutes or hospitals, preferably dressed in simple black. . . .

"He did not like formal audiences. He wished to give his visitors all the time necessary to say what was on their minds. He would listen to them patiently and conduct the conversation informally. Even when he had to say no, he said it with great gentleness but with equal frankness.

"Everyone remarked the humorous, pithy and anecdotal nature of his speech. He steered clear of the negative aspects of life and would head off any displeasing turns the conversation might take for either party—the speaker or the listener. Thus no one ever heard him say a single disparaging word about anyone, near or far. He took people as they are, as the saying goes, and he liked to find the positive side in everyone.

"He was fond of repeating that in pastoral work it was necessary to 'See all, to pretend to see less, to correct a little,' in accordance with the proverb that 'Too many laws discourage the public.' And he said that 'One should only command those things which one can have a reasonable and solid hope of seeing carried out.'

"He would rise from his desk to receive visitors and always personally accompanied them to the door. . . . He did not like applause. He made this known from the pulpit of St. Mark's on his arrival in Venice by recalling the sadness of St. Pius X on the day of his coronation in St. Peter's when unrestrained and unwanted applause broke out about him.

"He always respected his collaborators, trusting them completely and encouraging them in their work. He listened to their suggestions sympathetically and understandingly, never, however, failing to evaluate them carefully. . . ."

Will John XXIII become one of the great Popes in history? Only the future may answer this question. But as of today, having witnessed the first acts of his pontificate, one can see that it holds promise of being "enlightened and glorious," as his Secretary of State Cardinal Tardini has said, and above all that Pope John will truly be a father and a shepherd.

Pius XII left to his successor the example of a saintly life and the increased prestige of the Catholic Church, a prestige due to his position and his personal, enlightened and resolute words and actions in defense of the dignity of man and the rights of religion. He also bequeathed him a treasure-house of doctrinal teaching that will appear always more precious the more that it is studied.

Together with these great bequests, John XXIII's predecessor has left him problems of extreme gravity and complexity, posed by the times themselves. He has left him the problems connected with the Church's struggle against Communism, the problems of racism, of the effects of nationalism on missionary action in former colonial countries, of special conditions in nations that have long been Catholic but in which materialism and indifference to the supernatural have replaced religion.

Pope John XXIII is well aware of these problems. And the spirit in which he intends to meet them was indicated at the time of his coronation when he said:

"We have at heart in a very special manner Our task as Shepherd of the entire flock. All the other human qualities—learning, diplomatic perceptiveness and tact, organizing ability—can succeed in embellishing and complementing the reign of a Pontiff, but they cannot in any way serve as substitutes for this. The central point, therefore, is the zeal of the Good Shepherd, ready for every sacred undertaking, no matter how daring. . . .

"Of greater interest than mere action in itself is the spirit of that action. Every pontificate takes on a particular feature from the character of the person who represents it. And certainly the features of all the Popes who succeeded each other down through the centuries are reflected and must be reflected in the face of Christ, the Divine Master who trod the paths of this earth for the sole purpose of spreading its beneficial teaching and His great example as summed up in His words: 'Learn of me for I am meek and humble of heart.' Hence the features of great meekness and humility."

After his election, Pope John XXIII did not take his name alone in memory of the father who had set him an example of a humbly but strongly lived Christian life, not alone in honor of the church in which he was baptized and of all the other churches dedicated to the Precursor, but above all because it was one of the names most frequently assumed by Popes. His desire is to be *Il Papa*—the father, the shepherd and nothing more. He did not set an ambitious program for himself by citing any of his predecessors, renowned for doctrinal profundity, intellectual attainments, or great deeds. It is useless therefore to seek for his model among the twenty-two pontiffs named John who have preceded Angelo Roncalli to the Chair of Peter. John XXIII has no idea of imitating any one of them.

The new visible Head of the Church has made known his desire to be father and shepherd not only to his sons within the fold of the Church but to those who are outside, and for that reason even dearer to him. It will be recalled that in his first message delivered to the cardinals on October 29th, and again in his Christmas message, the words of the Pope were directed to both the Western and the Eastern Church and to all those who are separated from Catholicism. He himself emphasized that the reference was not only to dissident Orthodox and to Protestants but also to those who were not Christian.

In the sentiments he expressed he showed a respect for the freedom of the individual soul. In them he also made clear his love of truth and of one's neighbor, and the conviction that the greatest benefit that can be bestowed upon a brother is to communicate the truth to him with gentleness and in a truly fraternal spirit.

A few days after his election John XXIII asked the *Osservatore Romano* to publish an address on the duties of a bishop which he had delivered on November 25, 1957 at the thirtieth diocesan synod in Venice. Making his own the ideas of his "dear friend" Archbishop Guerry of Cambrai, Cardinal Roncalli stated that the bishop must avoid two excesses: authoritarianism and paternalism.

"Authoritarianism in truth suffocates life, confining it within a rigid, outer discipline that is complicated and burdensome. It arrests legitimate initiative, it does not know how to listen, it confuses harshness with firmness, inflexibility with dignity.

"Paternalism is but a counterfeit of fatherhood. It keeps watch over others only in order to enforce its authority to govern. It is liberal toward some, but it does not respect the rights of its own subordinates. Its tone of speech is patronizing and it does not accept collaboration.

"The true fatherhood of the bishop, on the other hand, is shown by a respect for the rights of souls. It shows a ready disposition to develop in its sons the true and holy freedom of the sons of God. It is filled with goodness toward all. It acts energetically and forcefully against all those things that can enslave souls to passion. It foresees and forcefully denounces errors, dangers, and illusions. In its relations with the faithful it knows how to unite trust with prudence, firmness with compassion, and patience with decision."

Anyone is sadly mistaken who thinks that the Pope can adjust truth to the demands or caprices of men, that he can enter into pacts with error, or alienate even to a minor degree the precious patrimony of the Church of God. Therefore with him there will be no appeasement, but action in the spirit of true peace proclaimed by the angels in Bethlehem. The leaven of this action is prayer and the spirit of true penance, as he reminded his Venetians in his 1957 pastoral letter. Truth, he further said, is not supported by cold pronouncements but by bearing witness—that is by action.

In view of these traits of heart and mind all questions as to whether John XXIII will act as a "political" or a "religious" Pope, whether his views are Leftist or Rightist, appear futile. They are questions that can be asked only by those who see the Church as an earthly institution or whose desire, more or less hidden, is to yoke him to this or that ideology.

But, it is clear, John XXIII intends only to be Pope, that is, the just and loving Father of all. If there are those who do not recognize this—because the Cross is ever a sign of paradox and contradiction—it is nevertheless apparent in his life and actions and is recognized by his loving children and by men of good will everywhere.

Appendix

Here and there references have been made to the historical research of Angelo Giuseppe Roncalli, and to his works in ecclesiastical history. Following is a list of all his writings:

Il Cardinale Cesare Baronio, per il centenario della sua morte. Monza, 1908.

La Misericordia Maggiore di Bergamo e le altre istituzioni di beneficenza amministrate dalla Congregazione di Carità. 183 pp. Bergamo, Società Editrice Sant'Alessandro, 1912.

In Memoria di Monsignore Giacomo Radini-Tedeschi, Vescovo di Bergamo. 485 pp. Bergamo, Società Editrice Sant'Alessandro, 1916.

Gli Inizi del Seminario di Bergamo e San Carlo Borromeo. Historical notes with an introduction on the Council of Trent and the founding of the first seminaries. 87 pp. Bergamo, Società Editrice Sant'Alessandro, 1939.

Padre Maestro Giuseppe Caneve dei Frati Minori Conventuali. A eulogy delivered on May 31, 1943, at his funeral in the Basilica of Sant'Antonio in Pera. 24 pp. Padua, Tipografia della Provincia Patavina di S. Antonio, 1943.

Congresso Eucaristico Nazionale, Turin, Sept. 6–13, 1953. 280 pp. Ed. U.C.D. 1954 (Roncalli, A. G.): *L'Eucarestia fonte di solidarietà e pace sociale.*

Gli Atti della Visita Pastorale di San Carlo Borromeo a Bergamo (1575). Edited and annotated by Angelo Giuseppe Roncalli in collaboration with Pietro Forno. Vol. I, pt. 1: *La città*, pp. lvi + 416 (1936): vol. I, pt. 2: *La città*, pp. 561 (1938); vol. II, pt. 1: *La diocesi*, pp. xii + 690 (1939); vol. II, pt. 2: *La diocesi*, pp. 600 (1946); vol. III, pt. 1 (1949); vol. III, pt. 2 (still to be published). Florence: L. S. Olschki, and Bergamo: Società Editrice Sant'Alessandro (1926–1949). (Fontes Ambrosiani, in lucem editi cura et studio Bibliotecae Ambrosianae, moderante Iohanne Galbiati, vol. XIII–XVIII.)

In Memoria di Francesco Vistalli. Con uno scritto di A. G. Roncalli. 100 pp. Bergamo, Edizione Banca Popolare, 1954.

La Basilica di San Marco in Venezia. 303 pp. Venice, F. Ongaria, 1956.

His most important research was in connection with the publication of the *Atti* of the pastoral visit of St. Charles Borromeo to Bergamo in 1575. He himself describes them as follows:

"I first came upon the documents and correspondence relative to the apostolic visit of St. Charles Borromeo to Bergamo in 1908, at the center of the archiepiscopal archives in Milan. I was immediately struck by this collection of thirty-nine volumes bound in parchment on the back of which was printed: *Archivio spirituale—Bergamo.* I examined them, and I returned several times to go through them even more thoroughly. It was a pleasant intellectual surprise to find that such interesting and copious documents had been collected and arranged together. They dealt with the church of Bergamo during a period most characteristic of the renewal of her religious life, on the morrow of the Council of Trent during the most fervent period of the Catholic Counter-reformation. I decided then to publish the documents, employing, naturally, standards of the latest scientific scholarship and modeling myself on the best modern publications."

The project was encouraged by many authoritative persons. Mons. Achille Ratti (later Pius XI), in particular, heartily approved it and showed great interest in its progress.

Index